OUR STORIES GOD'S GLORY

Inspiring Testimonies of God at Work in Everyday Life

Compiled

Seed Faith Books

All proceeds from sa... go towards distributing books for encouragement and inspiration, given through HEART GIFTS 501(C)3

Thank You!

With love and appreciation, we thank all of you who shared your stories so others could be encouraged.

It's been our great joy and privilege to receive these *treasures* you've written. We've been strengthened in our own walk with God as we've listened to you.

None of you received payment for your story. Neither have we been paid for working on this book, so it has truly been a labor of love on everyone's part.

In Jesus' Name, all of us send these "seeds" forth to bless every reader.

David & Helen Haidle

Special THANKS to:

Elsie Heuerman, Patti Nelson, Susan Krueger, and Joanne Valiando for suggestions and contributions in editing and organizing these stories, and to Kelly Cutler for editorial assistance.

Portland, OR 97281 - www.seedfaithbooks.com
For more information, contact: helen@seedfaithbooks.com

Printed in the USA.
ISBN# 60101-059-1

Foreword

This inspirational book focuses on the loving, wonderful, and often miraculous ways God works in the lives of people today.

In this era of economic down-turn, governmental corruption and mismanagement, increasing crime and natural disasters, plus all the negatives that bombard our daily lives, now more than ever we need "good news."

The Good News for Christians is that Jesus Christ not only redeemed us by His shed blood on the Cross, but He lives with us today. And He has given us great and precious promises we can hold onto and believe in tough times.

God sometimes works by His Spirit in miraculous ways. At other times, God's providential care guides us into just the right moment to receive blessings and insights.

Yet not all stories transpire or end as we hope they will. Unanswered prayers do not negate or contradict God's perfect nature. God wants us to trust Him regardless, for His love is infinite and unfailing. His will is always right and good.

"As for God, His way is perfect" (Psalm 18:30).

God wants us to know beyond any doubt that when all else fails, He is enough.

by Susan M. Krueger

Whose Stories? . . .
HIS Stories!

Everyone has a story—a story with the power to impact us in a special way. When an individual in this book shares what happened in his or her life, one central character always emerges: GOD—the God of the Universe!

Actually, all these stories are God's stories. God is the Giver, the Revealer, the Redeemer, the Encourager, the Forgiver, the Helper, the Rescuer, the Provider, the Savior and the Friend.

How this book got started:

In my early teen years, my mother taught me embroidery. While we sewed together, she would recount the inspirational stories of her life.

I asked to hear the stories over and over, especially how the Lord held my mother's hand at the lowest point in her life.

Forty years later, at the point of death, the Lord gave her a vision and told her: *"Not yet, Ella. I have work for you to do."*

Mother shared how an Assembly of God preacher prayed for my grandmother and she was instantly healed of a skin disease. Mother told how relatives in South Dakota gathered together Sunday evenings to sing hymns and pray as they struggled through hot summers, failed crops, and harsh winters.

Many times, I asked Mother to retell the story of the angel who appeared to my Uncle Johnny before he died of cancer.

Nearly all the stories in this book come from people we have known here in the Portland *(Oregon)* area for over thirty years. We know the integrity of each individual and we are convinced of the truth of these stories *(copywritten for "one time use" only by Seed Faith Books).*

As people have shared with us their experiences of God at work in their lives, we have discovered each story to be unique because our God, Creator of the Universe, never seems to do the exact same thing twice.

David and I have also known God to be real in our lives, as we've experienced His touch during 43 years of marriage.

Even working on this book has been a step of faith, similar to the step David and I took in 1988, when we sensed the Lord's call to spend a year writing and illustrating *The Lord is My Shepherd,* a picture book on Psalm 23.

Today, fifty-five books later, we hope these testimonies will encourage every reader to trust our faithful God.

Our love and prayers,
Helen (& David) Haidle

TABLE of CONTENTS

God Keeps Every Promise

Rainbows remind us: God is a Promise-keeper. All through the Scriptures, God encouraged people to recall His faithfulness.

They were to remember when and where God reached with love into their lives and worked miracles, even those common everyday miracles we sometimes take for granted.

"For all the promises of God
in [Christ] are YES,
and in Him AMEN,
to the glory of God through us."

2 Corinthians 1:20

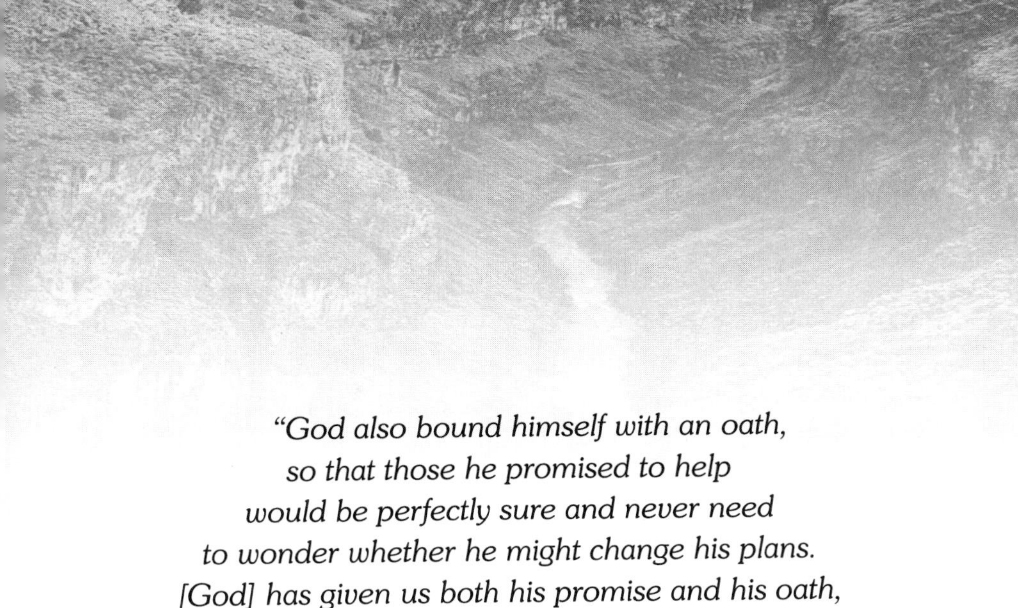

"God also bound himself with an oath,
so that those he promised to help
would be perfectly sure and never need
to wonder whether he might change his plans.
[God] has given us both his promise and his oath,
two things we can completely count on,
for it is impossible for God to tell a lie."
Hebrews 6:17-18 TLB

The following experiences of David, Randy, Patti, Otumdi, Joanne, Susan, Tom and others remind us of God's faithfulness to keep every promise in our lives today.

"He who has promised is faithful."
Hebrews 10:23

Windblown Seeds

Life holds many challenges for a self-employed artist. Yet every time my wife Helen and I prayed about quitting, we felt the Lord kept urging me to continue my art work.

But at this time, needing to provide for my wife and three small children, and with the challenges of working with galleries, I felt particularly discouraged.

Four of us men met together each Saturday morning for a time of fellowship. At the end of our meetings, we took time to pray for one another.

This Saturday, my prayer request was the same as always: for the Lord to guide me in my profession of painting and print-making, and to anoint me with creativity and skill like He had anointed Bezalel and Oholiab long ago (Exodus 31:1-6).

With my eyes closed, suddenly I saw a clear vision of a bush covered with small yellow flowers as Pastor Keith Reetz began to pray for me. The branches of the flowering bush gently swayed back and forth, blown by a gentle breeze.

Keith prayed that God would send my work forth like seeds, blown by His Spirit, across our land and eventually to many places around the world.

Keith ended his prayer by saying, "You know, that wasn't just *my* prayer. That was a *word of the Lord* to you."

"Yes, I know," I replied. "I was seeing a vision of everything you were praying."

Keith's face lit up. "I was just praying what *I* was seeing."

What an encouragement and confirmation—we were both seeing the same vision! When I went home and told Helen, we hugged each other and wept for joy.

Weeks and months and years went by. Keith's prophetic words had not come to pass, yet we continued to hold on.

My perspective changed over the course of time. Some things take a while. A long while, in my view. As time passed, I also realized the small blossoms in the vision had not gone to seed yet. And *seeds* only come from plants that have died.

Sometimes things need to die—dreams, plans, careers, or anything within our minds that must go through a transition.

God promised Abraham a son. Twenty-five years later, God fulfilled His word when Abraham was ninety-nine.

Now it's been over twenty-five years since Keith and I saw the vision, and I am getting old. But I do understand a little more how God has fulfilled and is continuing to fulfill this word to me. I've discovered that God's plans were bigger than I could possibly have dreamed up or imagined.

Over fifty children's books, as well as over 95,000 small pocketbooks and booklets my wife and I write and illustrate, have gone all over the world—from northern Alaska to the tip of South America, to many places in Mexico and Africa, and even to restricted places like Cuba, China, and the Middle East.

These Scripture "seeds" have been sent forth to children and adults I hope to meet someday in heaven.

About twenty years ago, my mother-in-law (who constantly prayed for my work) gave me this special Scripture blessing:

The Lord promises,
"I will instruct you and teach you in the way you should go; I will guide you with My eye upon You."
Psalm 32:8

David Haidle
Painter, Illustrator
Portland, Oregon
www.seedfaithbooks.com

Forbidden Shed

My hand trembled on the door knob of the old shed out back, my heart beat wildly, and my father's words boomed inside my head.

Yes, I knew what he had told me—

"Never go in the shed!"

But something inside me demanded to know why he had said it.

To a curious eleven-year-old child, the words "no" and "don't do it" are often not satisfactory, especially when the "why" is always answered with, "Because I told you so."

The door of the shed creaked open. Sunlight filtering through the shadows highlighted dusty cobwebs in an empty room.

Unfinished walls of roughly hewn two-by-fours surrounded me as a faint light glanced off a tuna can placed up high on a ledge.

Standing on tiptoes to reach the mysterious object in this forbidden shed, shame surged through my being and disobedience received its reward. Cigarette butts in a makeshift ashtray.

I knew I must never let my father know I had disobeyed him or that I had discovered his secret, but I did tell my stepmother. Her response was, "Well, now you know."

If she did tell dad, he never acknowledged my disobedience or discovery.

This was the year I accepted Jesus as my Savior, and now my nightly prayer to God was that He would help my dad quit smoking.

My father was a Christian, and to this child, a prince who could do no wrong. Yet, I felt it was my job to remind God that my father needed deliverance from this terrible habit.

Seventeen years later, God kept His promise and He answered my prayers!

Through discovery of a make-shift ashtray, God taught me to pray, even though the answer was delayed many years.

This experience has become a gift in my Treasure Chest Legacy because this is where I met God and learned to pray.

Jesus said, "*When you pray, go into your room,*
and when you have shut your door,
pray to your Father who is in the secret place;
and your Father who sees in secret
will reward you openly."
Matthew 6:6

Joanne Valiando, author
Treasure Chest Legacy Workshops
Treasure Chest Legacy Journal
Beaverton, Oregon

Give, and It Shall Be...

When I was in Bible college, I spent nights and weekends working at UPS and also for a local moving company. During that time, I felt the Lord call me to an early prayer time each morning, even though I wasn't getting to bed until the wee hours of the morning.

One of the things that came out of my prayer times was that God began to speak to me about giving.

Each month I worked enough hours to pay for my college expenses, plus I had about $40 left to buy gas for my car and to purchase those little necessities like toothpaste, etc.

One day, I was walking across campus with the $40 in my pocket and I saw a young couple from Uganda, whose church had sent them over here to prepare for ministry. I felt like the Holy Spirit nudged me to give them my $40.

As I walked towards them, I wondered if this was a test from God. Then I felt God say to me, "I want to demonstrate My love for them through you."

So I willingly handed them the $40 and said, "I just want you to know God loves you and cares for you."

As I walked away, I heard the young woman exclaim to her husband, "See! I told you God cares for us!"

Now I felt a real surrender. I told God, "All I have is yours."

That weekend, my roommate and I went to the laundromat. We jammed all our white clothing in one washer and all our darks in another.

Unfortunately, in the whites, I had left multiple ink pens in my pockets. The clothes all came out looking like they were tie-dyed. A couple of the grease pencils from UPS were in the load of dark clothes. What a disaster! In one afternoon, my roommate and I ruined all our clothing!

At that time, we were invited by a family at church for Thanksgiving dinner. During dinner, the woman asked me, "What's that spot on your sleeve?"

Well, we told the story of our ruined washing, and everyone laughed. But when we left their home, the couple gave each of us $100 and told us to use it for what we needed.

The day after Thanksgiving, I went shopping. After making some major purchases, I was standing in front of the Baskin Robbins counter and, out of the corner of my eye, I could see a speck of green lying on the floor—it was a $100 bill!

I quickly picked it up. Then, I waited there for fifteen minutes, watching to see if anyone came searching for lost money.

No one came, so I went to the information center and asked if anybody had reported that they lost some money. They told me no one had, so I could keep the money.

Shortly after Thanksgiving break, I received a letter from a family in Wyoming. They enclosed a $300 check and told me to use it for whatever I may need.

Now I felt the Lord prompt me, "Do you think you are going to do more for Me than I can and will do for you?"

I am not advocating that you give money away so God will give you more. But I do know from experience, that God's promises are completely trustworthy.

"Give and it shall be given unto you, good measure, pressed down, shaken together and running over."

Luke 6:38

Pastor Randy Remington
Sermon 7/18/2010
Beaverton Foursquare Church

Broken Vessels

At the end of the day, as my friend and I finished work on a small estate sale, I pulled some dust-covered boxes out of the attic for sorting.

Opening one box, I found a beautiful sea-blue crystal bowl etched in eggshell-colored swirls, with sparkling glitter-like gold detailing and with a scalloped rim.

The box must have previously been dropped, because as I picked it up, the base remained in the box. It was broken into two complete jagged pieces.

"It's too bad it's broken," said my friend. "This is probably French or Italian. Intact, it would be quite valuable."

She placed the bowl in the trash pile. I resisted the urge to pull it out, but after we left the house, I couldn't get it out of my mind. I was drawn to that bowl and its brokenness.

I've rescued many broken things and repaired them, or used the parts to create artistic objects. As I work on the broken parts, the Lord heals and works on the broken places inside of me.

I left the next day to take my elderly father-in-law on a Navy reunion trip. Relaxing on the plane, I pulled out a book about appreciating everyday miracles if you clear away the clutter and allow the Lord to nourish your spirit.

The significant symbol in the book was a bowl. The book told how, in some countries, broken bowls were mended by filling the cracks with a mixture of metal, chips and debris, mixed with glue. So when the bowl is repaired, you can see it was broken and is now whole again. These restored bowls became honored treasures.

As soon as the plane landed, I phoned my friend and instructed her to move the bowl from the trash heap to safety.

I then called my husband John and told him the story about the bowl and how I needed to save the bowl and repair it.

Upon returning from my trip, I retrieved the bowl and brought it home for repair. A few days later, I came home from working on the estate sale and there, sitting in the middle of the table in all its glory, was the bowl—repaired!

My husband had heard my heartbeat. Even though he isn't attracted to either broken objects or old things, he listened . . . and he repaired the bowl.

Chorus: *Something beautiful, something good.*
All my confusion, He understood.
All I had to offer Him was brokenness and strife,
But He made something beautiful of my life.

If I had any dreams that were lofty and noble,
These were my dreams from the start....
But my dreams turned to ashes, my castles all crumbled,
My fortune turned to loss.
And I picked up the pieces and laid them at the cross.

Chorus: *Something beautiful, something good. . .*

As the beautiful blue crystal bowl is my chosen treasure, so I trust God's promise that I am His chosen treasure.

The Lord said, *"He is a chosen vessel of mine."*
Acts 9:15

Patti Nelson
Hillsboro, Oregon

Invisible Helper

During the most difficult time in my life, my marriage was falling apart, my husband had lost his job, and we were forced to pack everything and move to Kansas to live with my sister and her family while my husband looked for work.

I felt totally devastated and all alone, unable to face any of it. I especially could not face packing our belongings.

One morning when I was supposed to be packing the boxes which were stacked in the middle of the living room, I was sitting at the kitchen table and crying. My mind reeled with fears of the unknown path ahead of me.

Suddenly, someone took hold of my hand and I felt such warmth and strength. I looked around, but the room was empty. I couldn't see a hand, but I certainly felt a hand holding mine. Just to make sure it wasn't my imagination, I squeezed my fingers together tightly. The invisible hand squeezed back.

Then the hand firmly, but gently, pulled me upward from my chair and led me toward the boxes waiting to be filled.

As I walked across the room, I felt someone walking beside me and I heard the swish of clothing at my right side. I stopped several times, to make sure the sound wasn't my own clothing.

With the help of my unseen companion, I was able to pack many boxes that day. The heaviness lifted and I could even sing hymns as I worked.

The next morning, I woke up feeling groggy. Remembering the difficulties I faced, sorrow flooded my spirit and my eyes overflowed with tears.

But once again, someone firmly grasped my right hand. Strength poured into my spirit. The hand held mine all day.

This happened again the next day and the next.

Four days later, when I'd finished all the packing, I no longer felt the hand. But now I was at peace. I knew God was with me on this unknown journey, and I knew I could trust God's promise to never leave me.

Thirty years later, I found this verse in Isaiah. It's exactly what God did during the dark valley of my life—He held me by my right hand, and I was no longer afraid.

I'm also convinced God holds my hand during every time of trouble and difficulty, even when I don't *feel* it, because I know I can trust His Word and promise.

"For I, the Lord your God, will hold your right hand, saying, 'Fear not. I will help you.'"
Isaiah 41:13

Ella Winckler Beckman
Mother of Helen Haidle
Mount Vernon, Iowa

Perfect Love

My body quaked uncontrollably the day I sat on our living room couch beside my husband, listening to my youngest son's announcement. "I'm going to Iraq."

Ray had earned two Purple Hearts in Vietnam and advised Tevin to avoid the military.

Tev had. He worked as an engineer for a company that made unmanned drone planes. Now he was headed to Iraq as a civilian.

"I'll be safe on a Marine base," Tevin assured me.

But as soon as he flew out, fear consumed me. I learned that eight-foot shrapnel-filled rockets exploded on Tev's base daily. Then Tevin told us about a mine he found one day when he left the base to retrieve a drone.

I awoke in the night praying for Tevin's safety. I worried through prayer all day long. I suffered until God spoke to me through the verse, ***"Perfect love casts out fear"*** (1 John 4:18).

God helped me understand I needed to love ***Him*** more perfectly. Love Him enough to understand He could protect my son as easily in Iraq as in Oregon.

Love Him enough to believe He held my son's future.

Love Him enough that if He chose for Tevin *not* to return home, I could accept it.

Tev returned home safely a year later.

Jeannie St.John Taylor, author
Culture-Proof Kids
Portland, Oregon

Miracle Baby, Miraculous God

At the age of twenty-nine and a young Christian, I was expecting my first child. Our baby girl's due date came and went, and the days dragged on.

When she was three weeks late, the obstetrician decided to induce the birth. It was as if Kristi was content to forever remain womb-protected. Safely delivered, my first baby was healthy and normal; I was a very joyful mommy.

Three years passed, and I still was not pregnant again. My husband and I grew impatient. We wanted our children to be close together in age. For several months, I took a fertility drug with no results.

Then, we attended the Basic Youth Conflicts seminar in Portland in the spring of 1974. It was the story of Abraham having Ishmael by Hagar and its sad consequences that the Lord used to speak clearly to my heart about not fully trusting Him. I repented of doing it my way and immediately discarded the fertility pills. Within three months, I was pregnant again!

But this pregnancy was nothing like my first. I had spotting in the first trimester, which my OB disregarded.

But I sensed something just didn't seem right.

In November, at 6 months along, spotting reoccurred; the doctor prescribed bed rest for a week. He intimated that this probably was just another "mid-term abortion".

I felt upset with the doctor and unsettled about this pregnancy's outcome.

During that period of bed rest, I was led to Jeremiah 32:27: *"Behold, I am the LORD, the God of all flesh; is there anything too difficult for me?"*

To this day I cannot remember how I was directed to this Scripture. But I claimed that promise, knowing God had spoken

 (Continued on next page)

comfort and hope to my heart.

The next Saturday morning, my water broke. My husband, an MD, immediately drove me to the hospital, muttering his unbelief in a favorable outcome.

Amazingly, I was not anxious. God's word from Jeremiah had settled my heart. I surrendered the outcome of this baby's life into my Heavenly Father's hands as He continued to pour out His unbelievable peace.

During that time in the hospital, another OB was covering for my doctor. The standard alcohol drip prevented contractions, but by Sunday evening, time had run out to keep the fetus in utero and my OB was called.

Just as labor was being induced, my doctor's son's asthma called him home and the attending nurse, a Christian, delivered our baby.

Katherine Jo was born alive at a mere two pounds, two ounces. They immediately whisked her away and took me to the medical ward.

The next morning, my neighbor and dear Christian sister Caroline, an ICU neonatal nurse, was the person who escorted me to ICU to see my newborn daughter.

Instead of fear and worry, all I experienced was great joy and gratitude that my daughter, this tiny mouse-like creature, was alive.

My resolve and God's peace remained; whether God took her or let us raise her was in His sovereign hands. It was my most difficult experience, yet God wonderfully sustained me.

I still am amazed when I remember all the miracles God performed for Katy Jo.

An unbelieving physician was prevented from delivering Katy, while loving Christians attended me and my daughter during and after her birth.

Even though Katy was left unattended for some time in the hospital corridor, she survived that unbelievable negligence.

She lived through the four hour ambulance ride to the University of Washington Hospital in Seattle.

She survived six weeks of serious illness, when daily reports told us she was just hanging on.

And the Lord performed a miracle in my heart by and through His faithful Word.

Katy is now almost thirty-six, a bright, normal woman who serves in the nursing profession.

I often ponder God's sense of humor: one child born three weeks late, one child born three months early, three years of waiting between my first two children, then getting pregnant three months after stopping the fertility drug, and finally, thirteen months later, my third child was born!

When we trust God for the outcome, there is indeed nothing too difficult for Him!

The angel told Mary,
"For with God nothing will be impossible."
Luke 1:37

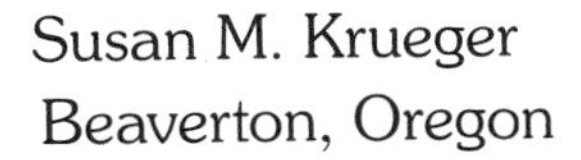

Susan M. Krueger
Beaverton, Oregon

Gift of Reunion

In the summer of 2009, while talking with my good friend Sherry Law, all of a sudden I experienced an outburst of prayer. My prayer surprised even me as I prayed that my sister Claire and I would be reunited. We had not seen each other for nearly fifty-six years.

When I was five-years-old, my father left our family and took a job in Alaska. Mother tried to find a children's home for the four of us girls. She ended up placing us in a juvenile detention home in Port Angeles, Washington.

Later we were transferred to the Seattle Children's Home. My younger sister and I were adopted by one family. My twin sisters Claire and Virginia were adopted by another family.

At this time, my adoptive parents had forbidden me to talk about my former family. This was very hard on me.

When I got a computer in 2009, I decided to put myself on Facebook. Amazingly, in August 2010, Claire's daughter found my Facebook account. She immediately emailed me, then phoned her mother.

At this time, Claire and her husband were driving from their home in Minnesota to Port Angeles, Washington, to visit our ninety-three-year-old uncle (our mother's brother). He had recently phoned my sister and said he would like to see all four of us girls before he died.

When my sister arrived in Port Angeles, she phoned me. It was a dream-come-true to reconnect with her. Then Claire asked if she and her husband could drive to Portland to see me before they returned to Minnesota. I felt overjoyed!

Just before Claire and her husband arrived at my house, I began to weep. This was very unusual for me since I had been told as a child that I was not supposed to cry. Now, all those old pent-up emotions poured out of me.

With all these wonderful reunions with my family, it almost seems like a dream.

Claire's children and teenage grandchildren want to get to know me, so now they email me, and I email them back.

Over the years, I had prayed fervently that Claire and her family would all come to know the Lord. Now, I am overjoyed to find out how God has worked in their lives.

The Lord has also been healing my past. As I have rested in the Lord and His timing, I am finally being reunited with my family.

What a reunion! Only God could have arranged all the details so wonderfully.

"I waited patiently for the Lord; and He heard my cry. He has put a new song in my mouth."
Psalm 40:1, 3

Beverly June Nelson
Beaverton, Oregon

God Didn't Give Up on Me

Through the influence of my grandmother, I accepted Christ as my Lord and Savior at the age of ten. But by the time I qualified as a Nigerian physician at age twenty-six, I had wandered away from God.

God patiently waited until I was thirty-two-years-old. At that time I was in private medical practice at Owerri, Nigeria, and my wife and I were parents of a baby girl. Then the Lord reached out to recover me.

First, my father died in 1981, and God let me see his lungs during an autopsy. What I saw caused me to immediately stop smoking.

My father's lungs were tarry black and shrunken from over thirty years of moderate smoking. I decided I could not let that happen to my lungs. I also quit drinking to help avoid my cigarette craving.

My wife and I had been regularly attending church after our wedding, without my having a serious relationship with Christ.

Then in November of 1985, we reluctantly honored a friend's invitation to a Full Gospel Business Men's Fellowship International breakfast meeting.

The testimonies and message we heard that morning were so challenging that my wife and I both responded to the altar call. A year later, I got baptized with the Holy Spirit.

I began sharing my faith with many friends, associates, and patients. After a while, I felt the Holy Spirit leading me to start my clinic with daily morning devotions in the waiting room.

Some of my out-patients received Christ during those morning devotions. My clinic staff followed up with all of our in-patients, some of whom even received Christ prior to their discharge.

We discovered God was faithful to keep every promise. Some of my new out-patients were touched with the healing power of the Word of God. They felt so much better after the morning devotions that they went back home without ever receiving any treatment at all!

I extended my gospel sharing to Holy Rosary Hospital Emekuku near Owerri, where I was also on staff. I prayed before every surgery, and I experienced God's guidance through many complicated cases.

In January of 1996, I had a dream that God was moving me to the USA for some specialty training. During the next seven months, my wife and I witnessed God's intervention on our behalf. We were able to get visas, and we arrived in the USA in July of 1966.

"[God] sent forth His word and healed them, and delivered them from their destructions."
Psalm 107:20

Otumdi Omekara MB.BS., MPAH
Consultant Medical Writer, USA
Medical Director Tumex Clinic
Owerri, Nigeria (1996)
www.droomekara.com

Answered Prayer

Nerves on edge, I listened intently to the newscast as the broadcaster announced that Desert Storm was about to begin and American troops would invade Iraq at any moment.

My husband and I knew that our oldest son Jeff, a marine, would be one of the first into action.

"Dear Lord, you know where Jeff is," I prayed. "Please be with him. Send a protective hedge of angels to guard him."

While I prayed, a picture flashed in my mind. I saw my son holding his rifle and lying close to the ground on a sandy hill. There behind him stood his guardian angel. *(I had seen this same angel stand behind Jeff once when Jeff was at our house.)*

Then I saw six more angels arrive and join Jeff's guardian angel, surrounding him like a hedge.

I praised God!

Shortly after the invasion, Jeff phoned us.

"Mom," he said, "I knew you were praying for me before the war began. I couldn't see them, but I could feel angels all around me!"

Judy Harris
Carleton, Oregon

Vision Fulfilled

Separated from my elk hunting party, I stood alone at the top of a mountain ridge in Eastern Oregon. I began to pray and weep before God with my hands uplifted in worship and praise.

Soon I could no longer stand, and I found myself laying face down in the pine needles. I'll never forget the quiet voice of God saying, "I have sent My servant to this church to do a great work. Hear him, learn from him, and watch over him."

Ron Mehl had just arrived to lead our Beaverton Foursquare Church. He spent the first month walking back and forth across the front of the church, praying. He said he was waiting for people to walk in the door as the Lord had promised him.

Five of us met for a church board meeting one night. We knelt in prayer to earnestly seek God's will and direction.

As I prayed, God gave me a vision of our church—it was overflowing with people. In the vision, God called out people by name, and both men and women stood up, answering His call to ministry.

At the end of our prayer time, Pastor asked us to stand and share. When I stood, I began to shake. My voice trembled. My legs got so weak, I thought I would fall down. I braced my right leg against the pew. I shook so badly, my knees hit one another.

This close encounter with God changed my life forever. No longer would I criticize anyone who fell to the floor after prayer or anointing with oil. And I knew God would fulfill this vision in His own time and way—which He HAS!

"'Not by might, nor by power, but by My Spirit,' says the Lord."
Zechariah 4:6

Tom Thompson
Portland, Oregon

Move that Mountain

When I was in junior high, my family lived in army barracks housing where I shared a small bedroom with my younger brother. My dad's teaching income just wasn't sufficient to buy a house.

One Sunday, our pastor preached on Jesus and the fig tree, and the words spoken by Jesus came alive to me:

"If you have faith and do not doubt,
you will not only do what was done to this fig tree,
but if you say to this mountain,
'Be removed and be cast into the sea,' it will be done.
Whatever things you ask in prayer,
believing, you will receive."
Matthew 21:21-22

The biggest *mountain* in my life was getting out of the barracks and into a house. So I began asking the Lord for a house . . . one where I could have my own bedroom with pink walls and flowered curtains.

For two-and-a-half years, I prayed in faith, trusting God to answer. I trusted God's promise so completely that when I got up in the morning, I would look out the window at the vacant lot across the street, expecting that God could even place a house there for our family.

In my naivety, I didn't think about the fact that if God did put a house on that lot, the home wouldn't belong to our family, but to the owners of the lot!

One day in May while grocery shopping with my mother, I saw a notice about the Pillsbury Bakeoff. I grabbed an entry form and took it home. I sent two recipes to the Baking Contest, but after I mailed them out, I forgot all about it.

In October, I received a phone call from the Pillsbury company informing me that I had been selected as one of twenty junior winners to go to New York City and participate in their annual bakeoff contest.

During the next two months, I practiced baking my cookies. But neither my parents nor I ever dreamed I would win any of the prizes. Not those plain little butter cookies with a fork mark. Mother and I considered it a great prize just to go to New York City, all expenses paid!

Baking my cookies in the Waldorf Hotel Ballroom was an incredible experience. The beautiful cakes, pies, and other fancy entries awed me. I wondered how I ever got there!

At the Awards Banquet on the day after the Bake-off, they announced the winners. I was stunned when they announced I had won the Junior Second Prize! I knew it wasn't because of my baking skills. This award was God's merciful answer to my fervent prayers.

Back in 1955, that second place award of $2,000 was just exactly the right amount for a down payment on a house. And the Lord brought along the *perfect house* that just happened to come on the market at just the *right time.*

The day of our move, my mother, brother, and I gathered around the piano *(another gift of God that came with the house),* and we all sang, while my father played the hymn, *Now Thank We All Our God.*

2nd Prize Junior winner
1954 Pillsbury Baking Contest

Helen Beckman Haidle
(Mount Vernon, Iowa)

God's Love and Care

"The Lord is my shepherd, I shall not want.
He makes me to lie down in green pastures;
He leads me beside the still waters.
He restores my soul."
Psalm 23:1-3

Jesus said, *"I am the good shepherd; and I know My*
sheep, and am known by My own. . . .
and I lay down My life for the sheep. . . .
My sheep hear My voice . . . and they follow Me.
And I give them eternal life,
and they shall never perish;
neither shall anyone snatch them out of My hand."
John 10: 14-15, 27-28

Where do we see evidence of our Shepherd's love and care in our lives today? And how do we share the love of God with others so they too can see Him?

Reflect on these stories from Ria, Jim and Arlene, Carolyn, and others, who share times in their lives when the Lord displayed His loving care to them, or when they shared His love with others.

Then, think about the evidences of God's love in your own life—in the past and in the present.

Notice how God's love often comes through another person used as His instrument.

The overflowing, unconditional LOVE of God gives us confidence to entrust our future into the hands of our Good Shepherd.

Patient Prayer

Marie, the first patient I found on my evening nursing rounds, was crying. A week ago, this same lady had cried a lot while she talked to me at length. The day nurse in her report had written that Marie had been weepy all day "as usual."

Last week, Marie cried as she told me she thought she was dying. (Although she is not dying at the moment, she is going downhill and her mental condition is aggravating the situation.)

Tonight, Marie was soaking wet from perspiration as she told me she did *not* want her planned surgery and she did *not* want a colostomy.

Knowing she was Roman Catholic, I asked her, "Did you have Holy Communion lately, Marie?"

"Yes," she said. "Yesterday."

"Marie," I asked, "do you feel close to God?"

Marie just shrugged her shoulders and began to cry.

I boldly said, "Let's pray about it now." Then, I prayed while Marie spontaneously repeated every sentence I spoke.

After praying, I sponged her off, helped her change into a clean gown, and put fresh linens on her bed.

The rest of the evening was hectic from my point of view, but Marie rested quietly, with no more tears. It amazed me how content she was all evening long.

This was the first time I had ever prayed with a patient, and I praised the Lord as I continued my work.

Ria Naito, RN
Beaverton, Oregon

Touch of Spirit

There it is . . . still smoking from a fiery crash! A blackened shell, the remains of a 727, lay in the center divider of two runways at the Venezuelan airport. Forty-nine people died!

The year was 1983. I was to report for a one-month United Nations hydrologic project in Caracas, Venezuela.

"I'm going, too!" my wife Arlene proclaimed upon learning of the assignment.

Preparations began, buying new luggage and summer clothes appropriate for the tropics, plus contacting our church secretary for names of missionaries in Venezuela. Much to our delight, the secretary informed us about a husband and wife team ministering in Caracas.

We prayed for travel protection, insight into my new job requirements, and also "hitting it off" with the missionaries.

The morning after we arrived at the Caracas International Airport, I went to the office of the Director of Venezuela's Natural Resources for a briefing. As the briefing drew to a close, the officer surprised me by handing me a check for the entire thirty–day assignment.

After stopping by a local bank to cash the check, I returned to our hotel.

"Guess what I've got in my briefcase?" I said as I emptied the case, full of paper Bolivars on the bed. We both laughed as we exclaimed, "How rich we are!"

Our richness was short lived. The next day, headlines on the local newspaper declared:

BOLIVAR DEVALUED . . . 58 PERCENT!

We quickly calculated it would be impossible to stay in Venezuela for the full thirty-day period.

 (Continued on next page)

"Touch of Spirit" continued . . .

We prayed, "Lord, lead us; give us direction."

The decision was to stay and work until the money ran out. After a discussion with the director regarding yesterday's devaluation, they agreed a shorter stay was acceptable.

A surprise awaited me upon my arrival from work!

Arlene had contacted the missionaries, and they had invited us to dinner. Leslie also said, "We know what the devaluation has done to us. It must have affected you the same. Gary and I will be making a two-week visitation to the back country churches. Because the house we live in is God's house, you and Jim can stay here while we're gone. So pack your bags and be ready to go when Gary comes to get you!"

Definitely a big surprise! "Praise God!"

That evening at dinner, the four of us hit it off, so much so that Gary and Leslie invited us to stay in God's house for the entire time of my assignment.

Now I could relax and concentrate on the project.

At the start of the third week of work, my colleagues informed me that the coming weekend was a national three–day holiday. The staff insisted I should also take Friday off and fly to the city of Merida in the southern Andes.

"Be sure to ride the cable car to the 15,000 ft. elevation," said one of the staff. "It provides a panoramic view of the Andes Mountains."

The secretary immediately telephoned AVENSA, the local airline, for a 10 a.m. Friday flight to Merida. She was about to call a hotel in Merida for a reservation when, suddenly, I felt a very strong check in my spirit and told her to change it.

Surprised, she replied, "I don't understand why you would take only three days off and not four."

"I want to work the full week on the project," I said. It was important for me to complete this job with integrity.

So for me it became a Saturday, Sunday, and Monday holiday. Plane reservations were made for a late Friday afternoon flight.

We had settled in the airport waiting room when Arlene suddenly elbowed me in the ribs.

"Hey! Why'd you do that?" I asked tersely.

Silently, with a concerned look on her face, Arlene directed my attention across the aisle to a man reading a newspaper. At first, I didn't comprehend why she wanted me to look.

Suddenly my eyes focused upon the extra large bold black headlines that screamed:

AVENSA INFERNO. 49 MUERTO.

(Avensa Airplane Inferno. 49 Dead.)

Later, as the plane Arlene and I were on continued past the smoking wreckage of the plane at Barquesemento Airport, I knew if it had not been for that strong "check in my spirit," we would have been on that 10 a.m. flight!

"Go near and listen to all that our Lord God says."
Deuteronomy 5:27

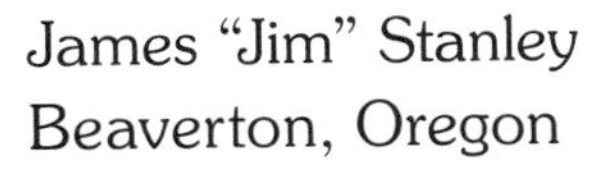

James "Jim" Stanley
Beaverton, Oregon

Christmas Shoeboxes

I love to spend time with my grandsons, Jacob (10 years) and Conner (6 years). I equally enjoy showering them with gifts.

When I heard about the Christmas Shoe Box ministry, I knew it would be a great opportunity for my grandsons to learn about giving to children who are less fortunate.

One afternoon, I took my grandsons shopping at the local dollar store. The boys enthusiastically gathered fun items to fill two shoeboxes for boys their own age. It was a moving experience for them to pick out something they wanted for themselves and then put it in the cart for someone else.

By the time they finished, they had enough stuff to overflow the two shoeboxes!

Then we bought practical items like combs, toothpaste, toothbrushes, and soap. It gave me the opportunity to explain how important these things were to children who lacked most of the daily essentials we take for granted.

We brought everything to my house, where we wrapped the shoeboxes in Christmas paper and wrapped the lids separately.

What fun the boys had filling up the boxes with their purchases!

That weekend, when we delivered the shoeboxes to the drop-off location, we were amazed at the stacks of colorful boxes that filled the warehouse.

Now, my grandsons excitingly added their boxes to the countless gifts which had been prepared for needy children all over the world.

My grandchildren and I have packed Christmas shoeboxes for several years now. It is still one of my most favorite times with my grandsons and they talk about it often.

This simple act of filling and wrapping one shoebox to give children who have no other Christmas gifts has provided a memory–making activity of serving others together in the name of Jesus.

I hope it will encourage my grandsons to serve and give generously in the future. My prayer is that both Jacob and Conner will always be willing to share God's love and care with many poor and needy children and adults around us and all over this world.

"The generous soul will be made rich,
And he who waters will also
be watered himself."
Proverbs 11:25

Carolyn Hanson
Jacob Bingham
Conner Bingham
Beaverton, Oregon

Father Knows Best

In June of 1979, because of going through a traumatic divorce, I had a dramatic, life-changing experience with Jesus Christ. My heart was filled with indescribable joy and I was a completely new and different person from that day forward.

I began to attend a nondenominational Christian singles fellowship. One day, I met with the group for an outing. Two new ladies joined us. Listening to them as they talked, I learned that one had been recently widowed, the other recently divorced. I was amazed at their different attitudes. One was soft and gentle. The other seemed bitter and angry.

The more I got to know Joyce (the soft, gentle one!), the more I felt a great respect for her and her faith in God.

Eventually, Joyce went on a date with another guy in our group, but she dropped him fast! Then another man seemed interested in her, but for the wrong reasons.

I realized Joyce was naive in the ways of the world. My fear was that someone might con her. She did not deserve that.

But Joyce didn't even like me! She had made it very plain to everyone that she would ***never*** marry a divorced man.

Some time later at our singles meeting, Joyce confided in me what jerks her dates had turned out to be.

"Who do you think I should date?" she asked.

I thought for a few seconds. "Well, I don't know," I said, "but I'll tell you what I'll do. I'll roam around and talk to all the eligible guys. I'll see if there are any here I might recommend. Okay?" Joyce seemed to think that was fine.

For the next three meetings, I did just that. Finally, Joyce came to me and asked, "Well, what did you find out?"

I told her, "I talked to every guy here who is anywhere near our ages, and I'm sad to say that I don't think there is anyone here that would treat you the way you deserve to be treated . . . except me!"

"Okay," she said quietly, and then she walked away.

One night, I presented a Bible lesson for the group. After I left the podium and went to the back of the room, Joyce came up to me, put her hands on my shoulders, looked straight in my eyes, and said, "I love you!"

I had no idea what I'd said to elicit that kind of response!

"Whoa!" I told her. "Do you know what you are saying?"

Without hesitation, she nodded. "Yes, I do! Is that so bad?"

"Well, no," I said. "But we'd better talk about this."

After a heart-to-heart discussion, we decided to pursue a relationship to see where it could go. That was Valentine's Day, 1987. We married seven months later, on September fifth.

God took us through many changes—more for me than her—before our marriage really began to click. It took about four years before the light finally came on — WOW!

This marriage began for me with a new understanding of the word "respect" and quietly grew into a love I had not even hoped was possible. But our heavenly Father knew. He knows best. And He has made it work because of our commitment to Him.

Hanging on a wall in our home is this special plaque:

"As for me and my house,
we will serve the Lord."
Joshua 24:15

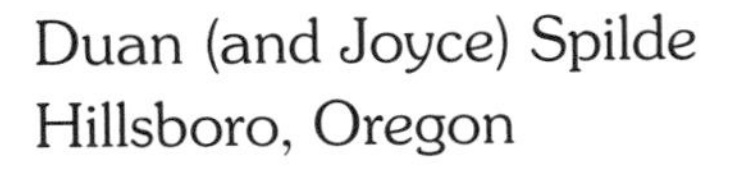
Duan (and Joyce) Spilde
Hillsboro, Oregon

Red Silk Pillow

At this time, our grandchildren had been taken away by the state because our son had been accused by his daughter Amy of hitting her while they lived at our house.

Now it was Christmas. Unable to have the grandchildren in our home, our party for them had to be held at Auntie Beth's.

As we left to meet Auntie Beth, who was bringing the children with her so we could all go together, I thought of the "I Love You" red silk pillow I'd forgotten.

I ran back and snatched it up with the thought, *Amy needs to know I love her.*

But in the car, the feeling that I was to tell her the pillow came from her Daddy, instead of me, rose up inside me. The conviction grew and wouldn't go away.

But what about me, God? Her Daddy didn't give the pillow to me to give to her! Wouldn't it be a lie if I said that?

Now the thought wouldn't go away and I knew it was from God. But what should I say?

Just say, "Jesus gave me this pillow and told me your Daddy sent it to you."

My fingers tightened on the pillow.

Okay Lord, I'll give it to her, but You have to show me the right moment.

An immediate peace fell over my spirit. With it came a deep joy. I was to be God's messenger to an eight-year-old girl with a broken heart.

When I arrived at the meeting place, I got out of our car and walked to over to Beth's van. Seeing Amy in the back seat, I looked deep into her blue eyes and smiled. "I'm so glad we can all be together to celebrate Christmas."

Amy's little lips quivered. "Except my Daddy can't come." Two big tears slid down her cheeks.

"I know honey," I said. "But your Daddy sent you a gift." I handed her the crimson silk pillow and said, "Jesus told me to give you this and tell you your Daddy sent it."

Amy hugged the pillow to her heart, gave me a shaky smile, then held the heart-shaped pillow high above her head as though she was showing Jesus she'd gotten her Daddy's message.

I fought back tears as she hugged it and traced the lace on its edges around and around.

She even wrote, "I love you," over and over in the steam, which clouded the car window.

Dear Lord, I'm glad You let me be Your messenger of love. Forgive me for wanting to have my own way.

Please take the many tears I've shed and make them into something beautiful. Thank You for giving a small child a red silk pillow. And thank You for Your love to bless my heart.

"[God] has made everything beautiful in its time."
Ecclesiastes 3:11

Eva Gibson, author
Forgiveness
Wilsonville, Oregon

Help Me, Lord!

Today was the dreaded day!

My dear daddy was coming to visit for a few days. But this time he wasn't alone. He was bringing along a woman he wanted me to meet.

I thought I was handling it pretty well until I saw his car pull up in the driveway.

NO! I cannot do this!

It had been only one year since my best friend—my own mother—had died of breast cancer. Sixty was too young to die.

Now what was I to do? I knew I must not cry, but my lip was trembling as I walked to the front door.

Resting my hand on the door knob, I prayed, *Please, Lord! Help me now.*

As I opened the door, I felt the Holy Spirit pour over me. His love, like warm honey, overflowed in me. His strength lifted up my down-cast spirit.

I knew the Lord was empowering me for this important visit. He enabled me to love this new woman in my father's life. And I'm happy to say that this love and power of the Lord worked in me for the next nine years, helping me love my father and his new wife to the end of their lives on earth!

"Call upon me in the day of trouble.
I will deliver you,
and you shall glorify me."
Psalm 50:15

Deloris "Del" Pike
Portland, Oregon

The Joy of Giving

For years I have worked as a "Santa" at Seattle's downtown Macy's store. I could write a book about my experiences! So many children have touched my heart and impacted my life.

I am especially happy when a child tells me, "I know that Christmas is really about Jesus. It's His birthday!"

I wholeheartedly agree with them!

Each year, several boys and girls whisper a request with tears in their eyes, asking me to please stop the fighting in their home.

Then, I gently explain, "I'm sorry to say Santa is not able to do that. But I know something you and I ***can*** do. We can pray for your parents. God is the only one who can change their hearts. And I'll ask God to help you trust Him in times of trouble, so you won't feel so upset."

One Christmas in 1999 when I arrived to work the morning shift, I saw a box for "Santa's Letters." Now, in all the years of my work at Macy's, there has never been a place to deposit letters from children. Ironically, the box remained there for only one day. It contained only one letter that had been left the night before.

The letter read: "Santa, as hard as I try to get along, my older brother and sister fuss about everything I do or say. I have become the kind of person I don't like. But all I want is for my mother to be happy. And, if you deem me worthy, I would like to have some art supplies."

With some help, I was able to track down what family had been in the store and had a photo taken the night before. I discovered they lived close to one of my rental properties.

First I went to a store and purchased a nativity set for the whole family. After I bought a variety of art supplies, I wrapped them up and asked Bonnie, my renter, to deliver them.

 (Continued on next page)

"The Joy of Giving" continued . . .

On Christmas morning, Bonnie drove to their house, left the packages at the front door, and then quickly drove away.

Every year at Christmas, I would purchase more art supplies and gifts to leave for the girl and her family.

The girl began sending letters to Macy's, thanking Santa for her art supplies. She wrote about the art classes she took in school and said she dreamed of becoming an artist.

She was impressed that someone gave her something for which she could NOT return the kindness or even say thanks in person.

Several Christmases later, Bonnie asked the family if they would like to meet their "Santa."

When my wife and I met with the girl and her family, the mother explained how, at the time of the letter, life had been very difficult for her youngest daughter.

"I need to tell you," she said, "that your secret Christmas giving transformed our whole family."

She also added, "The nativity set we first received is what we set up at the beginning of every Christmas season."

When we met in person, the teenage girl gave me several pictures she had painted. She apologized that she didn't have any frames for them. When we left that day, I gave her money to buy frames for the rest of the paintings she had done.

Over the years I have maintained contact with the girl and her family. From the first time we met them until the latest meeting, I could tell the family was getting along better.

At our last meeting, I asked the girl (then nineteen years old) what I could do for her.

She said, "I pray that you will find some other child and give to her like you have given to me."

It touched my heart that she wanted to have other children to be able to experience this secret giving also.

"Secret giving" affected all of us during those years. Even Bonnie, my renter, was greatly blessed to be part of it.

At first, Bonnie just laid the packages at the door and left. As the years went on, she waited until they answered the door and, as "Santa's helper," she took time to talk with them and find out how the girl was doing with her art.

I used to complain to the Lord, "WHY did You give me all this white hair when I'm only in my forties? Why so early?"

But when I began working as a Santa Claus, I understood. The Lord had a special job for me to do, and oh, what a great privilege it has been to love His precious children!

Jesus said, "*When you do a charitable deed, do not let your left hand know what your right hand is doing, that your charitable deed may be in secret; and your Father who sees in secret will Himself reward you openly.*"
Matthew 6:3-4

Robert "Bob" Eldridge - Seattle, Washington

Amazing Move

By January of 2005, I was totally burned out at my job, with my friends, with working, and with life in general.

I worked nights in a hospital Medical unit. My job involved a lot of walking, lifting, and bearing the weight of others.

My right knee had given me trouble for several years and now every limping step caused a grating, gravely-type pain. As 10 p.m. approached each night, the heaviness inside me grew unbearable. I didn't know how I was going to make myself go to work.

I prayed many prayers to my Father in heaven to help me make it three more months until my retirement. I asked God to help me through the next shift, to help me be a blessing to my patients and my coworkers, to not harm anyone, and to make good decisions.

At the end of February, I called the ortho surgeon's office to see if something more could be done for my pain.

Dr. Coen's assistant said, "How about surgery on Friday?"

Well, in thinking about it, the time would never be better, financially or job-wise. When other things fell into place, I called back and said, "OK."

After surgery on my leg and a few days of therapy, it was time to be discharged. I was doing too well to be sent to rehab, so they decided to send me home, even though I lived alone.

I was definitely not happy about that prospect. But my dear Heavenly Father blessed me with a friend who took me to her home for two weeks of recovery. She'll never know how cared for and loved that made me feel, not just by her, but by God.

The end of March, I went back home and my aunt came to help me transition. Another blessing from God.

In April, my niece in Seattle told me about a relative's art show in Portland. She asked if we could meet there and have dinner together.

After viewing the art, we all went out to eat. To my niece's chagrin, her husband's father, her uncle, and another friend tagged along with us.

Soon, nine of us were sitting around a long table, with their friend Randy Jelen sitting on the opposite end from me.

In quiet conversational tones, I told my niece (who was sitting next to me) that I was thinking of selling my home in Albany and moving to Beaverton where my son lived.

At the other end of the table, Randy heard me and he asked, "Can I come see your home? I'm looking for a home to buy in Albany."

He came, he saw, he liked, he bought!

Because of my recent surgery, getting my place ready for a new owner was an overwhelming job. But Randy gave me all the time I needed. He even helped get rid of some things and he hauled scrap metal to the salvage yard!

Friends and family helped me get packed up and, miracle of miracles, I arrived in Beaverton on July 1st.

"The Lord will perfect that which concerns me; Your mercy, O Lord, endures forever."
Psalm 138:8

Sharon Godsey. RN
Beaverton, Oregon
Parish Nurse

Lady Star - the Gift

"Do you think Grandma would let me have a puppy while I'm here?" Gail had asked that question fourteen years ago. I thought of it now as I held our faithful dog's head while the vet prepared to administer a shot that would end her life.

We'd had Lady for fourteen years. Two months ago, the vet told us she had incurable cancer. But Lady Star wasn't only a family pet. She was a gift from God, used in a most dramatic way in our lives.

My mind went back to 1975 when, at age fifteen, our daughter Gail had become a chronic runaway. Involved in an increasing downspiral of lifestyle, our heartbreak and fear for her safety intensified.

Just before we went to get her at the third juvenile detention center in less than a year, we knew something drastic had to be done.

Knowing my husband's parents go to Arizona every winter from their home in Portland, Oregon, helped form our plans. We would try a change of environment. I would take Gail and stay in their house while they were gone.

In the trunk of the car were two hastily packed suitcases, Gail's and mine. Due to an airline strike and it being the Christmas season, we had to drive 220 miles to find a flight with two available seats. At the airport, our good-byes were strained and tearful as my husband Jim and our eighteen-year-old son Greg put us on the plane.

Moments later, at twenty thousand feet, I was flying away from my home, family, friends, and my husband. Beside me sat this unruly, silent, stranger of a daughter.

"I was doing O.K. Why are you doing this?" she asked in a rebellious tone of voice.

Trying to keep my voice under control, I said, "We felt we had to do something."

With a toss of her head, she turned toward the window. I leaned back and tried to relax, but my mind kept returning to unpleasant memories of the last few months:

Not knowing where she was.

The painful, long distance call in November with my tearful question, "Gail, are you coming home for Thanksgiving?"

The evasive answer.

The watching and waiting as the day passed without her.

The detective we hired to find her as we grasped at straws.

Thoughts and questions whirled in my head.

Jim and I would be six hundred miles apart. How would this separation affect our marriage? How would we handle the loneliness? Would this "last ditch" effort even work?

At the Portland airport, Mom and Dad Stanley picked us up. It was the middle of December and they decided to delay their trip so we could all have Christmas together. Jim flew up and planned to help his folks drive south after the holiday.

Trying to keep a semblance of normalcy under these sad circumstances, Christmas lights and decorations were retrieved from the attic, along with the nativity scene for the mantle. As Jim's mom began baking, the same delicious aroma of happier Christmases filled the air.

Gail, her grandpa, and I walked over to the nearby shopping center to pick out our Christmas tree.

Seeing a pet shop, we went in to look at the animals. We wandered about, admiring the fish and watching kittens chase each other. I laughed at their antics and glanced over at Gail.

 (Continued on next page)

"Lady Star" continued . . .

Gail's face was lit up as she watched a puppy dance around in its cage. It was a reddish-brown spaniel-terrier mix, with white on her face, chest, feet, and a white tip on her tail.

"Isn't she cute?" Gail asked excitedly. "Do you think Grandma would let me have a dog while we are here?"

"You'll have to ask her when we get home," I replied.

We carried the Christmas tree home and Gail led the way with surprising eagerness in her step. We'd barely set foot in the door when Gail rushed to find her grandmother.

As they talked in the living room, we overheard Jim's mother answer, "It's really up to your mom, since she will probably have to clean up after the dog."

My mind was thinking paper training and chewed slippers. But, somehow, I knew this was important. So Grandma and Grandpa bought Gail the puppy for Christmas.

Gail named her dog "Lady Star." Enraptured with this lively bunch of fur, Gail even bought a dog training book.

One day as I leaned down to pat Lady Star, Gail exclaimed, "No. Don't pat her that way!"

Holding the training book in her hand, Gail informed us we were not to pat Lady Star on top of her head, but should stroke or scratch her *under* the chin.

She explained, "I want a dog that will proudly hold her head high rather than lowering her chin for a pat."

Privately, I wondered if the pride she wanted for her puppy was what she secretly wanted for herself.

The day after Christmas, Jim and his parents left. January second, Gail enrolled in high school and we both enrolled for counseling.

Each day after school, Gail would rush home and ask, "What did Lady Star do today?"

Then I would share Lady Star's newest antics.

One afternoon, Gail asked, "Mom, what do you think about my getting a part-time job?"

My heart skipped a beat as I realized the implication of this question. This was not the question of a chronic runaway! This was a question from a girl making plans to stay.

I had never known from one day to the next if Gail would come home after school or after an evening out. This turmoil eased when I realized that, while she could run away anytime, she knew her puppy would never survive on the road. Gail was changing because Lady Star was so very important to her.

Now fourteen years later, we watched the vet prepare the needle. My husband put his arm around me and said, "Go ahead, Doctor. Lady Star has earned her rest."

I said a silent prayer of thanks that Jesus put a special life-changing love in Gail's heart for this dog. And I felt at peace as I realized we were simply returning the ***gift*** to the Giver.

"If you then, being evil, know how to give good gifts to your children, how much more will your Father who is in heaven give good things to those who ask Him!"

Matthew 7:7-8, 11

Arlene Stanley
Beaverton, Oregon

Gail & Lady Star

Under Burnside Bridge

Every other Friday night, Beaverton Foursquare Bridge Ministry went downtown to serve the homeless under the Burnside Bridge.

Several Portland churches joined together to provide food, clothing, blankets, as well as Bibles. People also came to serve the homeless by washing their feet and cutting their hair.

Last time I went downtown to serve, I asked my ten-year-old grandson Jacob if he would like to go along with me. He agreed to join our group.

It was a very cold night in December when we bundled up and drove downtown to serve the homeless people.

When we arrived, we were given a choice of different work jobs. Jacob selected "Disney-Duty."

So they handed us two brooms and dust pans to pick up after people in order to keep the whole area as clean as possible during our time of service.

Three hours later, Jacob and I climbed in the car, turned the heater on high, and headed home.

"Nana," asked Jacob, "did you see the mom and dad with three little children? They all went back to the food table several times. And I saw them stuff as much food into their back packs as they could. Why did they do that?"

"Oh, Jacob. Do you realize how blessed you are?" I asked.

"What do you mean, Nana?"

"Well, you and your brother have plenty of good food and clothing, as well as a warm bed. Tonight those children probably ate the only good meal they'll get all week, and they will no doubt sleep somewhere out in the cold tonight. And probably tomorrow night, too. Being homeless is very difficult. I'm sure you don't think much about food and clothes, or even a bed, because your parents provide you with all you need. Maybe you sometimes take those things for granted."

Jacob sat quietly as we rode home. I could just see his young mind working as he thought about everything he had experienced that night under the bridge.

When we arrived at his house, Jacob told me, "Nana, thank you for taking me with you tonight. I want to go help downtown again. And I'm going to be more thankful for everything I have."

I hugged him with tears in my eyes.

"I agree, Jacob. I want to help downtown again, too. And I want to be more thankful for all the gifts God has given me. I'm also very thankful you went with me tonight. I love you, Jacob. Let's continue to serve the Lord together."

"He who has pity on the poor lends to the Lord,
and [the Lord] will pay back what he has given."
Proverbs 19:17

Carolyn Hanson
Jacob Bingham
Beaverton, Oregon

Heaven's 911 Rescues

Our God is a God of the impossible.

In faith we trust God, even when circumstances and events stop us, challenge us, or don't turn out the way we would like.

And when the unexpected happens, we want to call upon the Lord in the day of trouble, and we give thanks to Him, even in the midst of a crisis.

Sometimes traumatic circumstances do require a "rescue." When you read the following testimonies, be awed and encouraged at how God intervened in unique ways in the life of each person.

Rejoice at the ways in which they experienced God's help at critical points in their lives.

"Call upon Me in the day of trouble;
I will deliver you,
and you shall glorify Me."
Psalm 50:15

Rejoice with Nyla as she experiences God's special gift of resurrection on Easter morning.

Praise God for the dramatic deliverances of Pastor George, Rebecca and her family, and Jerry and Jan, from what would have been certain death.

Let Geneva, Jennie, Sarah, Bill, and Kara strengthen your faith and prepare you to deal with challenging experiences in the future.

Just like in the Scriptures, the stories of these "saints" are meant to encourage and uplift us. They also move us to praise and worship our gracious God of love.

Easter Sunday Miracle

My husband Ed and I drove through bright sunshine from our home in Beaverton, Oregon, to Salem.

My sister Rosemary and her husband Gordon were waiting for us so the four of us could attend their Salem Foursquare Church together.

It was Easter Sunday. I loved the hymns we sang in church that morning: "The Old Rugged Cross" and "He Arose, He Arose, Hallelujah, Christ Arose."

Pastor Cox had just begun his sermon when I looked over at Ed. I was stunned to see his eyes wide open as he stared straight ahead. His head and features were stiff and unmoving.

I shook Ed's arm and spoke his name, but there was no response from him.

I nudged my sister and whispered, "Look at Ed!"

She looked as frightened as I felt.

I had to get help for Ed and quickly. Maybe there was someone in church with medical knowledge who could help.

I stood up and it seemed to take forever for the pastor to look in my direction.

"Is there a doctor here?" I asked.

"No," he said, "but I am here."

With those words, Pastor Cox left the pulpit and came walking down the aisle with long strides. Standing in front of us, he gently placed his hands on Ed's shoulders and began to pray.

I have no idea what he said. All of my attention was on Ed.

At first there was no change in Ed.

Then slowly, slowly, I saw life come back, first into Ed's eyes and then in his face.

Then, the sweetest smile I had ever seen was on Ed's lips.

Later, after the service ended, one man who had been sitting near us told me he had been in the medical corps in the Army. He said that when a person's eyes are open and fixed like Ed's eyes had been, the person does not come back to life.

Amazing Grace.

Amazing Love.

God, in His goodness and mercy, gave Ed and me our own "Easter miracle" that Sunday morning. (And that's exactly what Pastor Cox wrote in the next Sunday bulletin.)

"Jairus came and pleaded with Jesus to heal his little daughter. 'She is at the point of death,' he said in desperation. 'Please come and place your hands on her and make her live.' And Jesus went with him . . . and healed her."

Mark 5:22-24

Nyla (and Ed) Booth
Author: *Room for One More*
Beaverton, Oregon

Unexplained Exit

One hot summer day, when my high school buddy and I went for a drive, I stopped my car at an intersection of two country roads in Kansas.

All of a sudden, an approaching truck charged across the intersection and headed straight towards my car. I just sat there, shocked and paralyzed, unable to react!

The next thing I knew, I was standing in the road beside the rear end of my car.

In unbelief, I stared at the truck. It had totally crushed the left side of my car, where I'd been sitting in the driver's seat.

When I could finally move, I rushed to the passenger's side of my car to check on my friend. I found him pinned between the dashboard and his seat. Although he was badly shaken, he seemed to be unharmed.

I breathed a sigh of relief. But when I glanced over at the driver's seat, I could hardly believe my eyes.

The front end of the truck had totally crushed the entire driver's seat.

If I had been sitting there when the truck barreled into my car, there is no way I'd be alive today.

The force of the truck's impact rammed the steering wheel completely through the front seat all the way into the back seat!

When the police and an ambulance arrived, everyone asked me the same question.

"What happened? How in the world did you get out of your car without opening the door or a window?"

I didn't have an answer. Since the car's air conditioner had been turned on high, I had rolled up all the car windows. The windows were still rolled up in spite of the bashed-in door, which they had to pry open.

Neither my buddy nor the truck driver could offer any explanation for how I got out of the car.

Between seeing the truck barreling towards me, and when I found myself standing unharmed on the road next to the trunk of my car, I couldn't remember one single thing.

Everyone who witnessed the accident scene knew there was no logical explanation for how I exited my car before that crash.

"For [God] shall give His angels charge over you, to keep you in all your ways."
Psalm 91:11

Rev. George Dikeman
Beaverton, Oregon

Midnight Collison

Jerry: In March 1997, my wife Jan and I drove our Priva van (with a large glass windshield in the front), pulling a fully loaded trailer from Sisters, Oregon, to an art stamp convention in Southern California.

We decided to leave late at night to miss the winter storm moving in the next day. After driving through Klamath Falls around midnight, we came around a bend in the road. As our headlights lit the long stretch of highway in front of us, we could see a herd of deer standing all across the roadway.

The deer stood frozen, staring at our headlights as we sped towards them at sixty-five mph. I slammed on the brakes, but I could feel the trailer pushing us forward.

Jan: I frantically searched for an open space where our van could drive through. But deer covered both sides of the highway. With the Priva windshield that comes down in front, we could clearly see the deer directly in front of us.

Jerry: I put my arm out in front of Jan to try and protect her. I knew I couldn't avoid hitting the deer or going through the windshield. I heard Jan scream out at the top of her lungs, *"Jesus, help us! Jesus, help us! Jesus, help us!"*

Jan: While I was screaming, we reached the herd, but we amazingly went right THROUGH the bodies of the deer!

Jerry: I brought the van to a near stop on the other side of the deer. Jan and I just stared at each other with our mouths dropped open.

I told her, "Jan, there has got to be blood and guts and hooves all over the front of this van."

Yet we never felt one thing! Not even the slightest nudge.

When we arrived at the California–Oregon border fruit inspection center just past a town called Dorris, we stopped where there were lots of lights and got out of the van. My legs felt like jello. We looked all over the front of our van, but we found nothing wrong, not even one scratch!

Jan: I can remember at the time, that if the windshield hadn't been there, I could have reached out to pet the deer in front of us as we seemed to go through the herd in slow-motion.

Jerry: I couldn't understand how we stayed solid and yet transparently floated through the deer as if they weren't there.

I was especially glad Jan was with me in the car, because if I had come home and told her the story of what happened, she would have thought I'd been smoking *whacky-tobaccy* again and had some kind of hallucination. Jan and I are so opposite. I'm the dreamer, the artist. She is rock solid. She has to *know* for sure something is real.

Both of us experienced a miracle beyond our imagination! If God had not intervened, we would have died or at least been seriously injured. I also realized there was no gap between the end of Jan's prayer and the start of the miracle. She cried out and God miraculously answered!

Soon after we got home from the convention, I sat down and opened my Bible. When I looked down, I saw the verse:

> *"[God] will deliver the needy who cry out."*
> Psalm 72:12 NIV

Jerry & Jan Werner
Werner Graphics
www.wernergraphics.com
Redmond, Oregon

Unexpected Surprise

When I was sixteen, my church went on a mission trip to Mexico. However, at that age, I wasn't exactly looking forward to this evangelistic outreach.

I knew it would be interesting to get to travel to Mexico, but I also knew this was for our church outreach, and at that time, I was struggling with my faith.

All my life I had been taught about Jesus Christ, yet now as a teenager, I found myself questioning my faith in Him. After thinking more about the mission trip, I decided to protest to my mother about going to Mexico.

Mother ignored my protests. "You're going!" she said. Somehow she knew God wanted me there in order to bless me.

When our group got to Mexico, the teaching and healing crusade lasted for three days, with hundreds of locals gathering in an old bull fighting arena.

Each evening, after my pastor preached God's Word, people had the opportunity to come up on stage to ask the Lord into their lives or to have prayer for healing.

Some members of our group (including myself) would stay in the crowd and ask if anyone needed prayer.

This is when I found a woman who had a large growth on her forearm. It was a tumor, about the size of an orange. I had never seen anything like that before. I remember thinking how painful it must be for her.

An interpreter helped me communicate with the woman as she told us her story. We found out she had lived with this tumor for three years as it continued to grow.

The woman told us she had gone to many doctors, but none of them had given her any diagnosis.

I took that to mean the doctors didn't know how to help her, or perhaps the doctors she had access to didn't know what was causing the tumor.

Then the woman began to cry as she explained why she felt so desperate. She told us, "If there is no change in the tumor in the coming months, the doctors are going to recommend amputation of my arm!"

So the interpreter and I laid hands on this woman's arm and started to pray. I remember holding my hands over the top of this overgrown tumor as I prayed to the Lord.

Suddenly I realized that, as we prayed, the growth seemed to be shrinking under my hands! It felt so crazy! I opened my eyes so I could see what was really happening.

Watching intently, the interpreter and I continued to pray as God removed this dreadful thing right in front of our eyes and made the woman's arm completely normal once again!

What an absolute miracle!

I have never doubted the Lord since. God proved Himself to me that day through a complete stranger and it changed my life!

"They cried out to the Lord in their trouble, and He saved them out of their distresses."
Psalm 107:19

Sara Sampaulesi
Scappoose, Oregon
with her mother, Linda Owen

Fixing the Accident Zone

All I can do is pray. Ever feel like that? I do, often.

That's the way I felt the day of the big crash on the curve near my home. Car wrecks there had become common. I'd prayed for crying passengers, tended cuts and bruises, and also called the police at times.

I had complained more than once.

"Drivers aren't sufficiently warned about this curve."

This time the sound of the crash shook the kitchen, and I went running. It was a car load of high school students on their way home—the long way home. A young driver, trying out his mom's new car, failed to negotiate the curve. He over-corrected himself on the wet pavement and slammed into a tree.

The young driver wandered around the road, dazed. Five girls screamed in pain, jammed inside the car.

Back to the phone I ran, called 911, called the church prayer chain, put hot tea in a thermos and hurried back.

"Lord, send the angels," I cried as I ran. "Lord, send the angels."

Other cars stopped. Someone helped one of the girls out of the vehicle. A lady comforted the crying girls. Another prayed for the girl behind the driver who seemed to be hurt the worst.

Moments seemed like hours as we awaited the ambulance. Since other people gathered around the car, I stood back and prayed. I prayed for their lives and for their salvation. And I kept praying, "Lord, send the angels."

People from a nearby home brought blankets for those chilling in the Oregon rain. And finally, the ambulance and fire trucks arrived.

One girl was taken by life-flight to the university hospital. Others went to the local hospital.

Days passed before I realized the Lord ***had*** answered my cry. Angels had come in the form of people—those who prayed with and comforted the girls, those who brought warm blankets, and, eventually, the emergency medical people.

Not enough could be done, though, and one girl died. She was a Christian, and the only one using a seat belt.

Shaken by the tragedy, I took around a petition for my neighbors to sign, asking the roads department to lower the speed limit, put in a speed bump, and give better warning.

I asked the high school to limit students driving to school to those who needed to drive themselves, and also asked the school to ban passengers in student-driven vehicles.

Not much happened, though the road department did put up an arrow, indicating the curve in the road.

I'd done everything I could. Disappointment set in. What else could I do? A girl lost her life. A family mourned. I didn't want it to happen again.

So this time I prayed, "Lord, send an angel. Station him on that curve. Prevent further accidents."

And, you know, that was many years ago, and there hasn't been a serious accident there since, to my knowledge. I thank God that praying brings the best results of anything I can do.

"Pray for one another."
James 5:16

Geneva Iijiama, author
Jesus Loves Us All
Oregon City, Oregon

9:00 a.m. Nose-Dive

In the early seventies, the Charismatic movement arrived with the "rush of a mighty Wind." Dr. Dennis Bennett, an Episcopal priest, had just published his book, *Nine O'Clock in the Morning.* (See Acts 2:13-16)

My wife Marian, just saved and born again, wanted more. A Christian friend gave her Bennett's book and also urged her to attend a Bible study on "The Infilling of the Holy Spirit."

I was still floundering in my walk.

(Definition: Not yet saved.)

I had attended a few Bible studies and charismatic church services, but all their teaching fell on my closed ears and stony heart.

One week, my business travels took me to Hickory, North Carolina, on business. I found a red-eye flight to Minneapolis on Northwest airlines, an early morning flight on Delta to Atlanta, and an afternoon flight on Piedmont Airlines to Hickory—PHEW!

Marian had urged me to read the "Bennett Book" as I called it. To appease her, I took the book aboard the flight.

I did read the jacket bio on Dennis Bennett during the red-eye flight.

As we headed to Atlanta on the second flight, I opened the book and began to read the first chapter.

Then the flight attendant announced, "When we reach our cruising altitude of 32,000 feet, we will start serving breakfast."

After she served my tray of food, I closed the book and laid it on the empty seat next to me.

Suddenly, without warning, the plane went into a steep nose-dive. We plummeted approximately 10,000 feet in a matter of seconds!

During the chaos, I remembered three things:

1. I saved my food tray from spilling all over the floor,
2. I was completely at peace,
3. It was Nine O'Clock in the morning.

A God–Thing, yes!

Well, I finished Bennett's book that day. My walk with the Lord had finally begun!

> *"For it is the God who commanded*
> *light to shine out of darkness*
> *who has shone in our hearts to*
> *give the light of the knowledge*
> *of the glory of God in the*
> *face of Jesus Christ."*
> 2 Corinthians 4:6

William "Bill" vanBaggan
Beaverton, Oregon

God is Faithful

It was after hours as I waited outside a business building in St. Petersburg, Florida. My co-workers were bringing the key so we could enter the building and do our cleaning for the night.

Since the building was located in an unsafe warehouse district, I had been instructed to wait *inside* my car until the other cleaners arrived.

It was very hot that night and I thought, "Nothing bad will happen to me," so I stepped out of my car to wait.

As I stood in the empty parking lot, a man suddenly came out of nowhere and stood in front of me.

"Is this your car?" he asked.

Out of habit, I quickly reached in my pocket with one hand to check if my keys were there. He saw me do this.

The Holy Spirit took over at that time and, as I looked the man straight in the eyes, I started yelling, ***"No! No! No!"***

I yelled this loudly many times in a row.

After what seemed like an eternity (but it was probably no more than a minute or so) the man quickly looked behind him and then ran off.

Even though I had *not* done what I was supposed to do, God faithfully protected me that night from any number of possible traumatic events.

"If we are faithless, [God] remains faithful. He cannot deny Himself."
2 Timothy 2:13

Kara Baker, author
http://captivatingdesire.wordpress.com
Beaverton, Oregon

Good Samaritan

Last summer, I traveled to Costa Rica for a trip that would change my life. I went to work with researchers in the field, collecting data on how to help coffee grow more sustainably. This was my first time in Costa Rica, so I decided to go a few days early to explore the capital city of San Jose and get settled in.

Little did I know that I would get to see more of Costa Rica than I ever bargained for.

The afternoon of my second day there, I got caught in one of the country's typical afternoon thunderstorms, which meant heavy rain showers that would last for hours. I stood on the street corner, chatting with some of the locals as we each tried to decide whether to wait out the storm under a store canopy or make a run for it.

After half an hour of waiting, I decided it was time to make a run for it. Traffic in San Jose is CRAZY! Pedestrians have no right of way. So I was very careful to check for traffic before crossing the street. I looked both ways, looked again, and then made a dash for the other side of the street.

As I got to the middle of the road, a big city bus barreled around the corner. I didn't see the bus until it crashed into me, sending me and part of its bumper flying to the ground.

The only thing running through my mind was, *"I hope he stops. I hope he stops."*

I took a mental inventory as I lay stunned on the ground for a few moments and then tried to rise to my feet.

Thankfully, many people rushed out to the street to help me walk to the sidewalk in safety.

Placed under a canopy to protect me from the rain, a crowd of concerned, caring people gathered around me, stroking my arm, bringing me water to drink, and making sure I was okay.

 (Continued on next page)

"Good Samaritan" continued . . .

In that moment I was very thankful for three people gathered around me who spoke English.

One was a physical therapist, who checked for any broken bones. Another called the police and ambulance. The third was a young man named Isaac, who spoke fantastic English and didn't leave my side.

It wasn't until I later retold the story to my family back home that I realized Isaac personified the story Jesus told of the Good Samaritan in Luke 10:30-37.

After the accident, Isaac stayed by my side to reassure me that everything was going to be okay. I was so thankful for his presence and his ability to speak to me in my language. His presence immediately helped me feel at ease.

He wrote down the name of the bus driver and his license plate number, and took photos of the bus. He purchased bottled water for me to drink and a bag of ice for my injured head while we waited for the ambulance to arrive.

Once the police and ambulance arrived, Isaac served as my translator, explaining what had happened and advising me on how to proceed.

My head needed stitches, which meant a trip to the hospital in my first ambulance ride. Isaac must have seen the apprehension in my eyes as I thought about taking an ambulance ride alone in a foreign country, and he offered to accompany me. When I arrived at the hospital, Isaac helped me get checked in and he chatted with me until they took me to be examined.

Then we exchanged goodbyes and I expressed my thanks to him, asking him if there was any way I could repay him.

Isaac answered, "Don't worry about repaying me. I know you would do the same thing if I were in your shoes."

While waiting to be examined by a physician, a nurse brought a note back to me on which was written: *"Jennifer, I need to go to my home, so call me when you can please. Take a taxi outside. Here's 2000 Colones. Isaac Gomez."*

I was stunned. In his amazing compassion, this young man had thought of everything, even providing money for a taxi ride back to the youth hostel where I was staying.

After x-rays, ultrasounds, and blood work, at last the hospital discharged me and I gingerly went out to find a taxi.

I was only back at the hostel a few moments before Isaac was on the phone, calling me to inquire how I was doing.

Now I was a bit more clear-headed, so I took the opportunity to ask him questions about the accident and to thank him for staying with me.

Upon my return home, I tried contacting Isaac numerous times, but with no success.

There is no doubt in my mind that God sent Isaac my way to support and care for me in my greatest moment of need.

"Though I am surrounded by troubles,
You will preserve me.
Your power will save me.
The LORD will work out
his plans for my life."
Psalm 138:7-8

Jennie Cournia
Beaverton, Oregon

Miracle Rescue

In March 2010, I wasn't sure why I decided to drive from Portland to visit my parents in Sacramento. I hate road trips and at this time I was eight months pregnant.

My husband Mike, unable to get time off from work, asked me to wait until later. I stubbornly said, "No!" as I piled my son Cohen (three-years-old) and my daughter Devyn (who had just turned one) into the van and headed to California.

After I unloaded everything at my parents' house that night, I found out my mom would be working all week. I wondered why I had driven there if we weren't going to have any time together.

I woke up on March 24th at 7:00 a.m. and heard my dad leave for work. Closing my eyes, I fell back to sleep.

When I woke up, I noticed black smoke pouring through the heater vent above the door. When I opened the bedroom door, I couldn't even see the other side of the hallway. Everything was murky black. Now I knew—the house was on FIRE!!!

I left Devyn in the playpen and ran to the back bedroom. When I opened the door to Cohen's room, it was filled with black smoke, but it seemed like someone was shining a flash-light on Cohen in his bed so I could see him.

I grabbed Cohen and ran to my brother's room.

"Rich! Get up!" I screamed. "The house is on fire!"

We got Devyn, but now we couldn't get to the front door. I knew we had to go out a window—but they were all locked!

Finally I got a window latch open and popped out the screen. The window sill was about four feet high, but I'm only 5'1" and there was nothing in the room I could stand on.

I tried to pull myself into the window, but I kept falling back. I worried I would hurt my unborn baby.

Glancing over at my kids and my brother sitting on the floor, their faces black with soot, I realized, *We are all going to die!*

The smoke grew thicker as I tried jumping and pulling myself up on the window sill, but I kept falling backwards.

Then I cried out to the Lord, "Please God! Help me get out! Help me save my babies!"

I am not sure what happened, but the next thing I knew, I was on the outside of the house! Frantically, I called to my brother, "Quick! Hand me the babies!"

My brother has a disease that affects his brain and all his muscles, so for him to be able to physically lift my babies up to the window sill was a true MIRACLE.

I grabbed the kids and set them on the grass as I screamed for help. My brother tried to pull himself through the window, but he kept falling backwards and hitting the floor hard.

When he finally got partway up in the window. Somehow, I grabbed him and yanked him out. He landed hard on the rocks below, but at least we were all out!

The fire completely destroyed my parents' house, but God had brought us out alive. God works through some of the roughest times to show us His mercies and love.

Also, because of going through the fire together, God helped me appreciate my brother and rebuild a relationship with him that had been severed several years ago.

"I am your God. I will strengthen you, yes, I will help you."
Isaiah 41:10

Rebecca (and Mike) Thomas
Cohen, Devyn, & Peyton
Beaverton, Oregon

Angels on Assignment

Angels watched and "rejoiced" with God during the creation of the earth (Job 38:4-10). God, who created the world, also created an invisible world we cannot see. Angels are part of that invisible world (Colossians 1:15-16, Psalm 148:2-6).

Millions of angels worship and serve God. They also serve the people who belong to God. Angels go where God sends them and do what God asks them to do.

The work that angels do is all about God, not about themselves. Whenever angels show up, all the praise goes to God, not to the angels, because it is God who has created them and sent them.

"I heard the voice of many angels around the throne
. . . and the number of them was
ten thousand times ten thousand."
Revelation 5:11-12

Why don't angels keep accidents from happening?

Remember what happened to God's own Son. An angel strengthened Jesus in the Garden, but angels did ***not*** save Jesus from dying on the cross.

Angels did ***not*** keep Daniel from being thrown in the lions' den, but God's angel was with him ***in*** the lions' den.

How can we be sure God's angels are with us, even when we cannot see them? Because God has promised:

"The angel of the Lord encamps around those who fear Him, and rescues them" (Psalm 34:7).

As you read the following testimonies of angels at work, praise God for His gracious work in the lives of Bill, Patti, Carrie, Shirley, Judy, Allen, Ron, and Joyce.

Angel on My Wing

During World War II, I flew a special P38 plane on daily spy missions to Germany from an air base in England. My plane was equipped with cameras to monitor enemy troop movements on the ground.

One cloudy day as I flew back to the base, the flight instruments on my plane quit working. I tried everything to keep the plane from stalling, but it tipped downward in a 500 mile-per-hour nosedive into the city of London.

My heart sank. I knew I was flying over a heavily populated area. Frantically, I tried to pull up the nose of my plane to stop its steep dive.

When the plane finally broke through the clouds about a hundred feet above London, it suddenly switched directions and headed back up in the clouds at a 45-degree angle.

I didn't know why the plane had changed directions so quickly—until I looked out the window.

I was astonished to see an eight-foot-tall angel in a long white robe standing beside the left wing of my plane. The angel's flowing robes and golden hair were completely unruffled and unaffected by the wind.

I didn't have much time to think about this since my plane's instruments still didn't work. But when the airplane reached a higher altitude, I knew I had to parachute out. I didn't have any idea what would happen to the plane or where it might finally end up crashing.

My parachute landed me in the backyard of an old London pub. The bartender, along with a crowd of people, came out to greet me with a tall mug of beer in his hands.

I graciously refused the beer, explaining that I didn't drink.

Soon a photographer arrived who took a picture of me and my parachute. Then, they helped arrange transportation for me to return to my air base.

The next day, my hometown newspaper in Portland, Oregon, printed that picture with an article about me on their front page. A friend saw it and took the newspaper to my wife. It was the first news my wife and mother had heard of me in many weeks.

I found out later that my plane crashed in another backyard, but no one was injured. I think it all was God's answer to the faithful prayers of my wife Harriet and my mother!

"God will give his angels charge over you,
to guard you in all your ways.
On their hands they will bear you up,
lest you dash your foot against a stone."

Psalm 91:11

William "Bill" Brabham
Aloha, Oregon
Entered God's Glory 1997
(Husband of Harriet Brabham)

Angel Intervention

For several years, my husband and I lived overseas in a Moslem country where he worked for an American oil company.

During that time, the Lord helped us meet a number of Americans who were Christians, as well as several former Moslem families who were secret followers of the Lord.

Bibles were forbidden and evangelism was declared illegal by this nation. Even though it was against the law to give out Bibles, we often carried Bibles and New Testaments with us to give to those we met who did not have a Bible of their own.

Since there was much persecution and imprisonment of Christians throughout the land, we had to be especially careful about taking Bibles with us when we traveled in our car.

Before every trip, we asked God to protect our travels, to keep us from accidents, and to guard the Scriptures we carried.

One day, we were driving with another Christian couple through a green light at a major intersection in a large city, when a speeding sports car suddenly approached us from the left.

Seeing the car come towards us at such a high speed, I knew a collision was unavoidable. My husband stomped on the brakes and I screamed as I lurched forward.

At the last moment, just before the car hit us, a very tall white-robed figure appeared out of nowhere, intercepting the car with strong outstretched arms.

The car came to a complete stop only a few feet from us.

As Paul and I stared in amazement, the powerful angel looked over his shoulder into our car as if to make sure we were all right. Then the angel disappeared from our sight.

My husband breathed a sigh of relief. "God's mighty angel definitely intervened on our behalf!"

I nodded silently, and praised God for His goodness in averting an accident and a potentially serious encounter with the local police.

Only God knows what could have happened to us if the stack of out-lawed Bibles in the back seat of our car had been discovered.

"The Lord is my rock and my fortress and my deliverer;
My God, my strength, in whom I will trust;
My shield and . . . my stronghold.
I will call upon the Lord, who is worthy to be praised;
So shall I be saved from my enemies."

Psalms 18:2-3

Patti Starr
Beaverton, Oregon

Carrie's Angel

When my five-year-old daughter arrived home from her first day at a new Christian school, she ran in the door and came to find me in the kitchen.

"Mommy," she said excitedly, "I saw an angel today in chapel."

I smiled. "You did? Was the angel a picture on the wall?

"No," said Carrie. "The angel was up on stage."

Puzzled, I asked, "Are you sure you didn't see a picture?"

"No, Mommy. He was standing right there in front of me—just like Mr. Jeffries was there."

Now I stopped washing dishes. "Did Mr. Jeffries see the angel?"

"Oh, no. He was talking to all of us kids."

"Well, what did the angel look like?" I asked.

Carrie thought for a minute. "He had a long robe. I couldn't see his feet." She stretched her arms up high, then flapped them like wings. Her face beamed. "The angel was real big. He was looking at me and he was smiling at me."

"Was the angel looking at the other kids, too?" I asked.

She shook her head. "No, Mommy. He just looked at me."

"Did the angel talk to you?"

"Oh, no, Mommy. The angel was *thinking* to me. But when I looked at my teacher and then looked back, the angel was gone."

She skipped off to play as I turned back to my dishes, thanking the Lord for Carrie's special angel encounter.

C. A. Hartnell, author
Scary Spring:
Our Polio Fright of 1955
First Book in a Four-Book Series
Henderson, Nevada

Not My Control!

My charming, blue-eyed son, developmentally delayed, does not normally sense impending danger. Neither did I as we drove home from bowling one sunny Saturday.

"Did you see that strike I made, Mom? I'm really good!" Paul beamed from ear to ear.

"Yes, you're good at bowling, Paul. Now, how about lunch?"

"Burger King?"

"Okay," I responded. Nearing an intersection, my eye caught a glimpse of a speeding car racing directly toward us.

"Oh, no!" Clenching my teeth, I gripped the wheel tightly.

Suddenly, an invisible force took the control of the wheel from my hands. I felt powerless!

Our car swerved violently, narrowly missing the oncoming car that flew through the intersection. Then, as quickly as it had left, all control of the wheel returned to my hands.

Shaking and weak, I managed to drive to the side of the road and stop.

"Paul, do you know what just happened there?" I asked.

"No, Mom, but I got scared!" he said.

"Me too, Paul. But God's angel took control of our car. The driver probably didn't even see us, but God did. I'm so amazed! We'd both be dead if it weren't for the angel's help. Let's thank God for saving our lives."

Paul nodded emphatically. We prayed, then headed home.

Shirley Dechaine, author
All About Me
One Family's Experience with
Smith-Magenis Syndrome
Tualatin, Oregon

Angel Biscuits

During World War II, I was among the American troops who were captured in Germany.

German soldiers forced us to march 100 miles, in snow and subzero temperatures, to another prison camp. During that long week, we received only two meals.

One snowy evening, as we trudged along the deserted road, I glanced up and saw a beautiful little girl standing beside the road ahead of us. She wore a winter coat with a fur-lined hood encircling her sweet shining face. In her hands, she held a small wicker basket.

As we marched closer to her, I could see her bright eyes smiling directly at me. She acted like she knew who I was, but I had never seen her before.

When we approached where she stood, she stepped up on the road and held her small, covered basket out to me.

As I walked to the spot where she stood, she pulled back the white napkin which covered the basket. I saw six biscuits inside.

I was so hungry!

Quickly, while still walking forward, I reached out, grabbed the six biscuits and stuffed them into my pocket.

The beautiful little girl flashed a radiant smile at me, and then she turned and walked away.

The other solders didn't seem to notice the girl. If any of them had seen the biscuits, I knew they would have desperately fought to get them. Everyone was so starved!

In fact, when we arrived at the next village, our captors let us sit down and rest on the street curb. A man wearing an apron came out from the bakery across the street and threw four loaves of bread into the middle of our troop.

Everyone jumped up, frantically pushing and shoving as they tried to grab a handful of bread. In their desperation and hunger, they hit and fought each other for every scrap.

I stood at the edge of the group and stared. I wondered why nobody had tried to grab the biscuits in the girl's basket.

Was it possible they hadn't seen the biscuits?

Was it possible they hadn't seen the little girl at all?

I can still see her beautiful face, even after all these years. It shone so brightly in the dusk. I've often thought of her. I had been too exhausted at that time to look back and see where she went or what happened to her.

Later, I realized no mother would have let a young girl take food to enemy troops at night during the middle of a war.

I believe she was an angel of God, sent as an answer to the prayers of my wife. Without those six biscuits, I would never have survived that week-long march in the freezing winter.

Jesus said, *"Your heavenly Father feeds [the birds], Are you not of more value than they?"*
Matthew 6:26

Allen Simantel, World War II Veteran
Simantel Berry Farms
Hillsboro, Oregon

Runaway Truck

While I waited on 87th Avenue for the traffic light to turn green so I could cross Canyon Road, my heart was full of praise to God for His forgiveness and mercy. The Lord had turned my life around. Now, I was serving Him.

When the light turned green, I drove into the intersection. A sports car drove towards me from the other side of Canyon Road and paused with its signals on, waiting for me to come through the intersection so it could turn left.

As I drove into the middle of Canyon Road, a sudden movement caught my eyes and I glanced to my left.

A large delivery truck was barreling towards me down the hill. But the driver's seat was empty!

I knew there was absolutely no place for the truck to pass between my car and the sports car. The front ends of our two vehicles were practically touching each other in the middle of the intersection.

I screamed as loud as I could, "JESUS!" and braced myself for the unavoidable crash.

But instantly, it was like the truck drove right through our two cars. It suddenly appeared on the right side of my car as it swerved into the opposite lanes on Canyon Road and crashed against a telelphone pole at the edge of the sidewalk.

Fortunately, there wasn't another car or pedestrian around at this time, so nobody was hurt.

I'll never forget the astonished look on the other driver's face as he stared at the crashed truck. I wish I would have taken time to get out of my car and talk to him. I would have asked him what he had seen!

(I found out later the truck driver had been delivering soda pop to a small grocery store on Canyon Road when the brakes of his truck failed.)

Stunned, I slowly drove the three blocks to my house, parked my car, and turned off the ignition. I closed my eyes and sent up a prayer of thanks to God.

As I was praising the Lord, I never expected God would show me why my car had not been hit by the runaway truck in that incident.

But, when I opened my eyes, I saw the reason.

There, on the hood of my car, sat a very large, powerful angel robed in white!

From that day on, the Lord has allowed me glimpses of the awesome and powerful angels He has assigned to help His children here on earth.

"Are [the angels] not all ministering spirits
sent forth to minister for those
who will inherit salvation?"
Hebrews 1:14

Judy Harris
Carleton, Oregon
(Lived in Portland, Oregon, at this time)

Was That an Angel?

One day during my flying career, I flew my F-84F turbojet fighter bomber out to a practice bombing range.

Because of the cloudy haze, I couldn't see the target very well from the normal start of 8,000 feet altitude. So I flew closer and finally spotted the target at 7,000 feet. As I rolled into my dive, I realized I was a little closer in than normal, and I also noticed that my dive was steeper than normal.

I knew instantly that I was in trouble. The target was too close and it was getting bigger! I was going in too fast!

I quickly started my pullout, but at 7.5 G's, the force was too much for the airplane. The whole plane began to shutter. It couldn't take any more. My heart sank.

My one thought was, "I'm leaving five kids!" I saw no hope of making it out of this dive. I estimated it would be twelve seconds from the time I rolled in until my plane hit the ground.

But the next thing I knew, the ground was dropping away from my sight and my plane was climbing steeply up in the sky!

My knees began shaking uncontrollably. I couldn't believe I was still alive! I should have crashed and been killed instantly.

I let the plane fly ahead for about twenty miles, without touching the controls at all, before I got up the nerve to bank.

I think God must have sent an angel to lift up my plane! He saved my life so I could get to know Him and serve Him.

"In their hands [angels] shall bear you up, lest you dash your foot against a stone."

Psalm 91:12

Ronald "Ron" Hanson
Major US Air Force (Ret)
Beaverton, Oregon

Freed from Fear

When I was about ten-years-old, my family lived in Tucson, Arizona. I learned to watch out for scorpions and black widow spiders who hid in dark places.

But snakes scared me the most! And I just knew snakes were lurking and hiding under my bed, ready to attack.

I was terrified of turning off my light and climbing in bed at night. So I figured out another way to get in bed and escape the snakes.

After I flipped off the light switch by my door, I went to the other end of the hallway. Then I would run as fast as I could to my room and leap into the safety of my bed.

One night, I suddenly woke up out of a deep sleep. There beside my door stood a glowing figure. I instantly knew it was God's angel, so I wasn't afraid. The angel's presence greatly calmed and comforted me.

I laid there, staring at the angel until I finally fell asleep.

Even though I never saw the angel again, I always knew it was nearby. And best of all, I never again was afraid of snakes underneath my bed.

Joyce Brabham Rose
Tigard, Oregon

Rough Waters and Dark Valleys

How are we to view discouragements, storms, and the trials of life? What helps us trust God today in the midst of rough water and dark valleys?

Remember Bible characters who had no control over the difficult circumstances they faced.

Joseph's brothers sold him into slavery, then Potiphar's wife lied about him. He ended up in an Egyptian prison. Yet God transformed Joseph's situation overnight.

King Jehoshaphat faced a hopeless situation when three enemy armies came against the nation.

Jehoshaphat prayed, *"O our God . . . we have no power to face this vast army that is attacking us. We do not know what to do, but our eyes are upon You"* (2 Chronicles 20:12).

The Lord fought the battle for them, defeating all the enemy armies.

In the following testimonies, we can be encouraged by what the Lord did for Joanne, Kara, Jim, Melissa, and others to bring them through dark valleys.

These stories remind us of God's ability to help us in the midst of depression, abuse, trials and storms . . . or even war.

Since God doesn't change, He can still encourage or rescue each of us as has been done to these writers.

"But now, thus says the Lord, who created you . . .
'Fear not, for I have redeemed you;
I have called you by your name; You are Mine.
When you pass through the waters, I will be with you;
and through the rivers, they shall not overflow you.'"

Isaiah 43:1-2

Confrontation

I had plenty I could say. Not usually at a loss for words, I was stymied and reduced to tears. My son is a master of logic and he knew just the right words that would shut me up.

Granted, living conditions were sparse at the moment, but it was a roof and hot meals. Two years before, my marriage had nose-dived in an ugly episode of domestic violence.

In a protective mode, I separated myself and my teenage son from the situation as I sought the Lord for answers. Five months later, I was in nursing school in a private, accelerated program.

Now, at forty-three years old, this late bloomer had a better way of providing for my household. All those years as a nurses' aide and the preparatory sciences had paid off.

We left Southern California for a smaller community and my son was okay with that decision, I thought.

As a night nurse, one of the dilemmas I faced was sleep deprivation. This was my emotional state when my son came into the house, awakening me mid-afternoon. Harsh words were exchanged.

In a terse voice, John's words caught me totally off-guard. "And what has God ever done for you, Mom?"

He knew the past—brokenness, faults and failures. He knew all our struggles and that I felt I had failed him.

Embarking on adulthood at nineteen, he spoke volumes in that one question.

I was speechless.

One night many years later, I was awake, my Bible open. I did not hear an audible voice or see a vision, but the internal nudge was clear and directed. *"Pick up your pen and write what I tell you."*

This type of an exchange with the Lord has only happened to me several times in my life. The first one was at the age of fifteen, the second one just before entering nursing school, and now.

Finally, God was giving me the answer to John's long-ago question, only it wasn't just for me.

That night, the idea of the "Treasure Chest Legacy" was conceived, giving every believer an opportunity to leave a written legacy of what God has done for them.

Scripture is clear. Share, tell, write down for present and subsequent generations what great things God has done for you. (Deuteronomy 6:6-9)

The Treasure Chest Legacy ministry has required me to go into deeper layers of repentance, relinquish judgmentalism, and seek the face of God as I never have before.

What has God done for me?

He has tuned me to His whisper and nudges.

What has God done for you?

Enjoy the adventure.

"Let this be written for a future generation,
that a people not yet created
may praise the Lord."
Psalm 102:18

Joanne Valiando, author
Treasure Chest Legacy
Workshops & Journal
Beaverton, Oregon

Our Difficult Experience of Parenting

I believe every parent feels that they have failed in some way with their parenting experience. We do the best we can with what we know to be the right way, and we have to leave the rest in God's hands.

My wife and I have parented four children, each one of them with a totally different personality. Yet, we felt we should treat them equally. As they grew up, we were challenged by their unique characteristics and traits.

One child was a strong leader, one was compliant, one was rebellious, and one was a sensitive peacemaker.

So… how do you handle and treat them "equally?"

Just recently, one of our offspring was going through yet another rebellious period in her life. We previously thought this rebellion would settle down as she grew up into an adult. That was not so. The rebellion seemed to rear its ugly head again.

We were at our wits end as we tried to counsel and advise her with our "elderly wisdom."

Yes, yes, yes. She heard what we said.

But our words went unheeded.

Finally, we were convinced that *we* were the ones who had totally ruined this child's life by not being good parents. All of this made us wonder how our God feels when we, His children, disobey and do not heed His word.

Recently, we were on our knees once again, begging God to change the attitude and behavior of our child.

How we anguished about our parenting, wondering if we had used the wrong words or maybe we should have been more forceful during her childhood.

Or… maybe we should have been kinder and gentler during our daughter's times of rebellion.

We were so hard on ourselves for not being convincing enough. No matter how hard we tried, we had been unable to change her.

Then one day God spoke very plainly to us and said:

"The work in this child is MY job, not yours.
You are to be an example of
My unconditional love and grace."

What a relief it was for us to hear these words!

Immediately, my wife and I thanked God for what will be the end result for this child.

We hope that we will see this happen in our lifetime, but we may not be that fortunate. Nevertheless, we know we have a faithful God. We can and we will trust Him for our child's future and for her salvation.

Anonymous

The Lord says, *"Fear not, for I am with you;*
I will bring your descendants from the east,
and gather you from the west.
I will say to the north, 'Give them up!'
And to the south, 'Do not keep them back!'
Bring My sons from afar, and
My daughters from the ends of the earth—
everyone who is called by My name,
whom I have created for My glory."

Isaiah 43:5-7

Dream Lesson

Dreams are nebulous things most of the time. We usually forget them as soon as we awaken.

This dream, however, has become a part of me. I have considered its meaning many times.

When the dream began, I was pushing a bicycle up a very steep hill. It was muddy and there was only a narrow track; actually it was more like a rut in a muddy road.

I had to stay in that track in order move a few steps at a time. The process was slow but, being determined to reach the summit, I finally achieved my goal.

It was worth the effort, for the view was lovely. The sun was shining and the air was crisp. There was a rolling, green meadow surrounded by trees.

The strange thing was what I was standing on. It appeared to be a viewing platform. As I stood there, I glanced down to the bottom of the deck and, much to my surprise, there was a large German Shepherd dog looking up at me. Beside him was a small creature that I guessed to be a weasel. This seemed very curious!

Suddenly, the small creature leaped straight for my throat. Amazingly, the big dog sprang right beside him, caught him in his mouth, and deposited him firmly on the ground.

At that point I awoke with a start. I immediately asked, "Lord, what does that dream mean?"

The answer came quickly. I'm sure it wasn't audible, but it was as clear as if it had been.

"That is how the Lion of Judah takes care of the evil one."

Meditating on the dream has convinced me that if you stay on the straight and narrow path, it will be a struggle, but the Lord will take care of you.

For some time, the image of the bicycle was a mystery to me, especially since I had never learned to ride one.

But then it occurred to me, as I thought about it, that the bicycle was really "*extra baggage*" that I need not have carried along with me.

Before His arrest and crucifixion,
Jesus prayed to His Heavenly Father on behalf of His followers:

"I do not pray that You should take them out of the world, but that You should keep them from the evil one."

John 17:15

Thelma Young
Beaverton, Oregon
Dream - 2009

Scars of War

The scars of war have faded on the terrains of battle where we fought during World War II on the island of Okinawa. But the scars on our hearts and minds will never fade.

These scars are embedded in our very souls: the images of our wounded and dying comrades, the adjustments to civilian life after the war with its many problems, learning to live in a wheel chair or confined to a bed, becoming blind, or enduring other handicaps.

I thank the Lord for my guardian angel who looked after me so that I emerged, in spite of some desperate situations in my 201 days of combat on Leyte, Philippines and Okinawa.

I had no significant impairment, only the scars in my mind and heart to contend with.

I was inspired by many acts of courage among the men who voluntarily gave up their lives so their comrades might survive.

I am thankful the scars of war in my mind and heart have faded (no more waking up screaming from nightmares with vivid images of the horrors I have seen)—faded enough to be able to carry on.

Girl on Okinawa

Wow! She was really something special!

I can't think of her even after all of these years without getting a lump in my throat and tears in my eyes.

It was the morning after the World War II battle that I saw her. A stream of Okinawan refugees was passing by our former front-line position.

The Japanese had been using them as human shields from our hostile fire. Now, the refugees were going to our rear area for medical treatment and food, and then to their homes.

In the distance, I could see her, a small girl, who looked like she was about eight-years-old, but she must have been at least ten-years-old. The Okinawans are small people.

As she drew closer, I could see that she was carrying a little boy on her back. I thought it must have been her brother. She walked with her elbows hooked under his knees.

As she passed by, I noticed her left hand had been blown off at the wrist and the sun had burned the raw flesh to a dark brown.

Think of how brave she was not to give up! Instead, she picked up her little brother who was unable to walk, and carried him.

I never spoke to this young girl, and I was not closer to her than ten feet, but I shall never forget her.

That little girl was an inspiration to me. She was a special example of self-sacrificing devotion, family love, and extreme courage.

"Greater love has no man than this,
than to lay down one's life for his friends."
John 15:12-13

Ed Booth
Beaverton, Oregon
Entered God's glory: April 26, 2006

Awarded a Silver Star,
two Bronze Stars, a Purple Heart
and other medals for showing
utmost courage during World War II.

False Expectations

After my gradeschool son and I spent time at a wildlife safari, we decided to drive to the coast for the rest of the weekend. Having no reservations, we prayed for a place to spend the night.

Before we left, the Lord spoke to my heart and simply said, "Trust Me." I felt God say the same thing twice on our way.

When we arrived at the coast, we drove up and down every street, but found only "NO Vacancy" signs everywhere.

As we searched, we drove by a city park. Glancing in that direction, Paul exclaimed, "Oh, look! There's Todd!" *(Todd was a good friend of Paul's. He and his mother were our neighbors.)*

I didn't think much of this, assuming Paul was mistaken.

I drove on relentlessly, but to no avail, searching for the non-existent "Vacancy" sign. Finally, I gave up and we headed home, feeling upset and disappointed.

Several days later, Paul discovered it ***was*** Todd whom he had seen at the park. Todd's mother told us they had rented a beach house and would have gladly invited us to join them!

Now I realized that, if I had not set my mind so firmly on God answering our prayers in a given way, I would not have missed His answer. We could have stayed at the beach and had an even better time, since we would have shared it with friends.

Since then, I try to lay down my own expectations of how God will answer my prayers. God's ways are so much higher than mine.

God says, *"So are My ways higher than your ways, and My thoughts than your thoughts."*
Isaiah 55:9

Tracy Sposito
Aloha, Oregon

God, My Refuge

I was born in Holland during World War II. In May 1940, the Germans attacked Holland. They bombed many homes, hospitals and government buildings in the country. Our family's home in Hoofddorp, near Amsterdam, was spared of any bomb damage.

As a mail carrier, my father rode his bicycle to deliver mail through the countryside. He joined the Dutch Underground and also delivered propaganda materials.

As a result of his activities in the underground, my father was wanted by the Nazis. Sometimes he would move from house to house of the other members of the Underground. He often ran through backyards and fields of his town at night. There were many months my mother did not know if he was even alive.

My father built a hiding place in the wall of his bedroom. He cut an opening in the wall close to the floor. The cut-out portion of the wall was covered with wall paper to match the rest of the wall.

After father was safely in his hiding place, my mother would push a large dresser in front of the wall to cover up this area. My father was 6 feet 3 inches tall, so this was an adventure to fit him into the hole in the wall.

My brother was five years old and I was three years old, so we were not allowed to know about this hiding place until the war was over.

One night, my mother, brother and I were upstairs sleeping in her bed. Suddenly, we heard a loud banging on our front door.

Mother ran downstairs where she discovered a group of Nazi policemen had broken down the front door. They were looking for my father and they kept asking Mother where he was. She stated over and over that he had left her and she hadn't seen him for months, but they wouldn't let up their intense questioning.

 (continued on next page)

"God, My Refuge" continued . . .

The police wanted information about where my father might be, so they tore everything out of the linen closet and threw it on the floor. They damaged other cupboards, looking for paperwork to implicate my father's connection to the Underground.

A large sauerkraut barrel stood beside my mother's bed. My father had put their personal papers in a waterproof container and placed it in the bottom of this barrel. The Nazi police never thought to look in the sauerkraut barrel.

All this time, my father was in his hiding place behind the dresser.

When the Nazis left, Mother did not feel safe to stay in the house. So she took my brother and me to my grandmother's house across the canal.

When we were at our grandmother's house, we were told not to go into her attic because she had "jewels" up there.

(Years later, my cousin told me that grandmother's "jewels" were actually JEWS she was hiding in her attic in order to save their lives.)

When my father came out of his hiding place, he climbed down the backside of the house on a rope. In the Underground organization, he had access to a policeman's uniform and false identification. So, in uniform, he rode his bicycle across town to go to my grandmother's home.

He was stopped by the Nazis and had to show identification, while they questioned him about where he was going. He could speak enough German to get through the checkpoint and was soon released to continue on his bicycle.

When he arrived at my grandmother's house, he put down his bicycle and pounded on her front door.

"Polici! Polici! Open up, open up!" he shouted.

Grandmother was startled to see a policeman at her front door. Looking again, she recognized her son and quickly let him in the house. We were all relieved to be reunited.

On May 5, 1945, Holland was liberated. I remember my parents dancing in the streets, celebrating the end of five years of war.

After the war, my parents decided our family would have a better future in America. They left behind all of their wedding gifts and the furniture my father had made. They were only allowed to bring two suitcases for all of us.

In July of 1947, we flew from Amsterdam to Copenhagen. When we arrived in Denmark, we found out we had no place to stay that night. Local police kindly let us sleep in the jail.

The next day we boarded a ship for America. Ten days later, the Statue of Liberty was a precious sight to see as we finally arrived in America.

Over the years, I have been so grateful for a loving God who spared our family during the war.

Here in America, God provided loving Christian friends and families to help us. Through it all, God has taught us that He will provide everything we need.

"I will say of the Lord, 'He is
my refuge and my fortress;
My God, in Him I will trust.'"
Psalm 91:1-3

Janette McWilliams
Aloha, Oregon

God's Gift of Renewal

When my television program was taken off the air and my clowning ministry folded, I slowly entered what eventually became a deep state of depression.

The shock of going from the "high" of tremendous success to the "low" of believing I had hit rock bottom, brought me to the point where I felt totally worthless.

All I wanted to do was retreat from life into my own private, black world that was enfolding me in a death lock.

Although I wanted to escape from people, my cherished friend, Charles Moore, made it a point to take me out to lunch once a week for months. He always picked up the tab, and he just sat, listening to me express my fears and confusion.

Wisely, he resisted the temptation to offer any advice. He realized I could not and would not hear him.

My family was drawn into the confusion. But what were they to do? How could they help me? No one knew.

It was excruciating enough to experience the fall to oblivion of my career. Life seemed so dark and desolate for me that I only wanted to hide under the bed covers, day and night, and never come out.

A few weeks after our Shekinah stage ministry closed down, I was lying in bed, thinking about how to put an end to my life. I thought suicide would bring everything to a close.

I had no idea how selfish it was to think only of myself in the situation. Nor did I realize the tremendous damage it would have done to my family.

That day, when I was lying on my bed contemplating suicide, I hardly noticed our youngest daughter, Desiree, open the door and walk to my side. Then, Desiree said something that shocked me back to reality.

"Daddy, wherever you are planning to go right now, will you take me with you?"

Her words pierced my soul. Through a flood of tears, I hugged and kissed her. God had spoken to me through her four-year-old lips, and brought my mind and soul back to life.

When I could speak, I told her, "God sent you to me for this very moment, Desiree. You are my special Angel!"

From that moment on, my life changed. I rediscovered my family and friends, and the love of our Lord Jesus flooded my soul once again.

I give all the praise and glory to our Lord, and my thanks to special friends and my wonderful family for patiently standing by me and going through it all with me.

God will heal a broken heart, but He must be given all the pieces.

"God has not given us the Spirit of fear;
but [He gives] power, and love, and a sound mind."
2 Timothy 1:7

James "Jim" Allen
"Rusty Nails"
Portland, Oregon

(See next page)

Epilogue—by James Allen:

After my battle with depression, the Lord lifted me up from my despair and carried me on in a far greater way than I ever imagined. I have retired from clowning, but I have gone on to minister in many churches in the Northwest.

Even though I lost most of my vision two years ago, I can't and won't let that stop me from sharing the love of God.

I am still giving messages at funerals and also in some Sunday morning church services, with the help of my wife and two daughters who read the Scriptures I use in my messages.

I want to encourage everyone:

Keep ministering,
no matter what happens.
God will help you.
He works everything out for our good!

God bless you!
Jim Allen
Portland, Oregon

Opening Doors

Out of the darkest seasons of life can come some of our best lessons. It has certainly worked that way for me.

God was there as I came out of a nervous breakdown to discover that my life was broken, and the people I cared about the most had been damaged by the choices I had made.

But God used the breakdown as a wake-up call, and the recovery process as a classroom to teach me how I had gotten to this point and how to avoid ending up there again.

Through the process, I noticed that I wasn't the only one who struggled with these issues.

Maybe our stories aren't all the same, maybe each of us has walked a different path, but there are some common threads that entangle many women and keep them bound, preventing them from living the free life that Jesus offers.

Even women who consider themselves Christians can have areas of their lives that they've never fully entrusted to God.

This is one of the reasons why I wrote my book, *"Are You Keeping a Secret?"* I wanted to help women begin to identify their own hidden areas of heart and mind and allow the Holy Spirit access to their soul.

"O Lord my God, I cried out to You, and You healed me."
Psalm 30:2

Kara Baker, author
Beaverton, Oregon
"Are You Keeping a Secret?"
www.winepressbooks.com

My Daughters' Prayers

My husband prided himself on the fact that he had his whole family "trained." We attended a Bible church, went to a small study group, and our children were in a Christian school.

One afternoon, I delegated different chores to our children, and urged them, "Hurry up, girls. We've got to get everything put away before Daddy comes home from work."

One girl took his shoes to put in our bedroom closet. In her haste, she tripped over the computer printer cord strung across the closet doorway to reach the outlet.

She cried out as the printer fell to the floor. I ran in and found the printer lid hanging ajar. It looked like it was broken.

Just then my husband arrived home. I knew I had to let him know, since his computer was *off limits* to me and the children.

Before even checking it out, he blew up in a terrible rage and began calling our daughter horrible names!

I ordered the girls to their room, intending to get them out of the line of fire and to a safe place.

Then my husband turned on me, yelling and calling me many degrading names. He raised his hand in the air, preparing to swing at me. The rage in his eyes looked like a wild animal.

As he swung his arm down to hit me, I silently prayed, "Dear Lord, I'm ready to meet you; please take care of the children." I just knew this blow could kill me.

I closed my eyes and tucked my head down to receive the blow. When I heard a loud crash, I looked up.

At the last second, my husband punched a hole in the wall instead of hitting me. It caused all our wedding pictures to fall off the wall and break into many pieces.

Angrily, he stomped off, got into the car and drove it wildly down the street. I never knew how long he would be gone or what mood he would be in when he returned. I just prayed.

Usually, when my husband returned home, he would act like nothing had happened. It was an unwritten rule these incidents were never to be brought up again.

But when he returned that evening, he came to me and said, "I don't know what happened. I had intended to hit you."

I'd never had the courage to respond to him in the past, but this time something supernatural took over and I said, "I know."

He frowned. "If I had hit you as was my intent," he said, "the blow would've killed you."

"I know," I replied quietly. Nothing further was said.

The next morning, I got him off to work, then woke the girls.

After the older girls left for school, my youngest child told me, "Mommie, last night when Daddy yelled at us and you sent us to our rooms, I got really scared. We all got in bed together and put the covers over our heads so we couldn't hear Daddy yelling. We prayed, 'Dear God, please don't let Daddy kill Mommy.' Then we fell asleep."

My daughters' prayers sustained me as I continued to walk through this valley of deep darkness, until finally I gathered the courage to make a healthier choice for me and my children.

"Thus saith the Lord that created thee . . . ,
'Fear not: for I have redeemed thee,
I have called thee by thy name; thou art mine.
When thou passeth through the waters, I will be with thee;
and through the rivers, they shall not overflow thee;
when thou walkest through the fire thou shalt not be burned.
For I am the Lord thy God, the Holy One of Israel, thy Savior.'"

Isaiah 43:1-3 KJV

Anonymous

Fulfilling Her Calling

I turned my life over to the Lord while in the middle of grief. My third pregnancy had gone much better than the previous two. No illness beyond the usual three months of morning sickness, and we'd reached my eighth month of gestation.

I was anticipating the Christmas gatherings with out-of-state family and our newborn baby.

Then, after a lonely Thanksgiving, I went into hard labor three weeks early. The labor and delivery were less than four hours. Tiffany Lynne had arrived.

For several hours I rested until the doctor came into my room and told me, "Your daughter has died." Then he added, "We have not lost a baby in over five years."

Months passed, tears flowed, searching prayers poured out with all the *"why"* questions.

The following summer I was again pregnant . . . and scared.

Friends shared their new faith experience and I wondered. I heard testimonies of the Lord meeting everyday needs.

Again I wept, but this time it was tears of relief, tears of hope, and tears of faith. In those first moments I heard in my heart: *"Tiffany fulfilled her purpose."*

Our baby's life was short and her ministry was completed when her parents turned to faith in the Lord Jesus Christ.

Jesus said, *"Come to Me, all you who labor and are heavy laden, and I will give you rest."*
Matthew 11:28

Dannah Taylor
Beaverton, Oregon

Blessing in Disguise

I was a typical teenage girl at age fifteen, doing well in high school, very much involved in my horses, with a busy social life. I was sure I had the answers to just about everything.

I had not dated very much, so when I met a young man who was a couple of years older, I thought I was in love with him.

In a matter of a few months, I made some choices that would affect my life forever. I felt nobody could ever love me as much as this boy was telling me he did, so I gave my virginity away.

By age sixteen, I was pregnant. When I told the father, he said, "I am ***not*** ready to be a dad."

So I found myself pregnant, alone, and very confused.

My doctor did a test on me that came back showing my baby tested positive for Down Syndrome. They immediately discussed with me the option of abortion, and for the next three months that's what the doctors encouraged me to do.

I went to Mexico on a missionary trip when I was three months pregnant. There, I witnessed a miracle that changed me and the way I believed in God. Now I knew God was capable of healing my baby and giving me a healthy child, so I went ahead with the pregnancy. Six months later, I delivered a perfectly healthy boy and, to this day, he is a blessing to me and to many others.

My son is a straight A student who loves to play his saxophone, ride quads, play soccer and hang with friends and family.

God is merciful and has His hand on us always!

Mother & Son

"To Him Who Believes"

My husband walked out on our family several times when our children were young. The last time he left, our youngest son Nick was fourteen years old. This total abandonment was so hard on Nick, and he turned to drugs, which became his life.

Nick ended up in jail a number of times during his teenage years. In September 2009, Nick returned home from yet another stint in jail. A few days after he arrived, he decided to go out one evening to meet a girl. He never returned home that night.

In my spirit I knew Nick was back on drugs again, but this time I felt an extra heavy burden.

I got on my face, alone before God, and I yelled, "Dear God, whatever it takes! Please, please save him!"

The next day, on all Portland's television evening newscasts, I saw photos of Nicholas. They reported on Nicholas' arrest, and stated that he was in the worst possible shape, near death, because of a drug overdose.

But from that day forward, God began His miracle process. Many times my pastor went to the Washington County Jail to pray with Nick before his sentencing.

I wrote daily letters to Nick and prayed almost daily with my neighbor, contending for his life.

Many Scriptures encouraged me to pray ***in faith.***

In Luke 1:45, when Elizabeth greets Mary and realizes Mary is pregnant with the Savior, Elizabeth tells her, *"Blessed is she who* ***believed,*** *for there will be a fulfillment of those things which were told her from the Lord."*

I knew I had to stand on God's Word and, in faith, believe the Lord's promise, *"Believe on the Lord Jesus Christ, and you will be saved, you and your household"* (Acts 16:31).

I was especially encouraged when I heard the evangelist Reinhard Bonnke speak at Portland University. He told about miracles in Africa, of a pastor being raised from the dead, and he said, "The more impossible the situation, the bigger the miracle."

As Reinhard Bonnke shared from Acts 26, especially verse 18, I realized God was speaking to me about the importance of MY faith. I knew that the faith *inside of me* would result in the miracle of my son's salvation.

Also in Hebrews, chapter 11—the FAITH chapter—Abraham knew that God was able to raise his son up, "even from the dead" (v. 19), and women of faith "received their dead raised to life again" (v. 35).

I have prayed fervently for my son over twelve years. Now thirty-two-years-old, Nicholas currently resides in an Oregon correction facility. At this time in prison, Nicholas has given his life to the Lord. He has been baptized and he has received the Holy Spirit. Now he's been chosen to help teach other inmates in the prison's drug program.

Only with God's Word could this have been accomplished. Nick is coming home in a few months and he is anxious to be truly serving our Lord.

"All things are possible to him who believes." Mark 9:23

Michaelita "Mickey" (& Nick) Wright
Beaverton, Oregon

New Year Focus

On New Years Eve, I was sitting and talking to a friend at church prior to the service, and I said something kinda off the cuff.

"I hope this year is a really good year, because last year really was stinking!" But as I considered what I said for a brief moment, the Lord immediately took me to task.

After I walked away from my friend, I found myself, at the Lord's prompting, just rehearsing & reviewing His faithfulness to me during the past year with all the things I had faced in terms of physical trials, along with other personal traumatic things that had happened.

In the midst of this, rather than focusing on the problems and trials, I realized God had been so faithful in all of it.

I knew God wanted me to turn my heart around. I had to repent. So, after the service, I found my friend again and told him, "I was out of line when I said what I did about last year being a stinking year. I realized God has been so good to me during the troubles of this past year!"

Now my conviction for this year is that I would be one who would demonstrate God's faithfulness on every front, in any opportunity I get.

I know that my joy is not dependent upon circumstances. It's dependent upon my relationship with God. It's dependent on being thankful for Him and for His faithfulness and goodness to me.

"Oh, give thanks to the Lord, for He is good!" Psalm 118:1

Pastor Harry Faulkner
Beaverton, Oregon

Drawing Close to God

When my husband and I woke up one morning to find our two-year-old son lifeless, it was a terrible shock.

I'd been walking my own path for quite a while, having lost touch with my roots, my spiritual self.

This traumatic event caused everything to come to a halt. My first reaction was to draw close to God. I knew I had to get to know God better, because my son was with Him. Drawing close to God helped me accept my son's death as I surrendered Kolby to his Creator and Savior.

This poem was a special blessing to me at Christmas.

Merry Christmas from Heaven

To mommy and daddy, and each special friend,
Someday we will all share God's life without end.
So please, dearest family, be thankful today,
I'm alive and still growing in a new special way.
I still share your hopes, your faith and your love.
Keep your eyes fixed on Heaven and all that's above.
Keep living each moment, alive in God's grace.
I came here before you to help fix your place.
I love you all dearly, now don't shed a tear;
'Cause I'm spending Christmas with Jesus this year.

Then God gave us a special gift. Lily, our baby girl, was born four days after Kolby's birthday, just one year later.

Melissa Meinz Manibusan
Sherwood, Oregon

Son: Kolby Styles Manibusan
April 1, 2003—May 3, 2005

Yet Will I . . .

"Though the fig tree may not blossom,
nor fruit be on the vines;
Though the labor of the olive tree may fail,
and the fields yield no food;
Though the flocks be cut off from the fold,
And there be no herd in the stalls—
Yet I will rejoice in the Lord,
I will joy in the God of my salvation."

Habakkuk 3:17, 19

When life's smooth circumstances turn into hell's torment,
If every dear relationship brings anguish to my heart,
Though catastrophic crises seem never to relent,
Yet hope will be my portion; joy will be my art.

If peace and blessed tranquility become a raging storm,
When everything that I hold dear decays before my eyes,
Though fairest fortunes fly away and need becomes my norm,
Ever looking heavenward, I'll claim His glorious Prize.

When economic promises turn into nagging need,
If hunger is my daily lot, to beg, my occupation,
Though nothing changes for the good, sore tempted to secede,
Yet I am His, and He is mine; oh joyous exultation!

Although the dreadest darkling clouds obscure my clear horizon,
Or catapulted from a cannon to land I know not where;
If never to be reunited, I languish in a prison;
Yet, I will sing praises and lift my thankful prayer.

Although my loved one's bitter heart never softens to forgive,
And sickness sends me to a grave untended and forsaken,
I will rejoice in God my King as long as I shall live,
No earthly loss or deprivation quells this consolation:

The Lord God is my strength and song, in Him I safely hide;
On highest hills where I am safe from sin's assaulting blows
I will on hind's feet gaily romp, and on His peaks I'll stride;
Whatever befalls me, this I know, in Christ I can abide.

Yet will I thus embrace Him more when lonely and afraid;
Yet will my glad rejoicing swell when consequence is sore;
Yet will I still believe my God to be my strength and stay;
Yet will I hold onto my Christ, and love Him all the more!

~Susan Mary Krueger
Beaverton, Oregon

Little "Hugs" from God

God's touch on our lives can be seen in the warmth of the sun after a long winter, a crocus peeking through the snow, music in the rain, the laughter of a toddler, the smell of freshly baked bread, finding what we've lost, etc.

We gratefully receive each little "hug" and all the special touches as from our Lord's loving hand.

When we keep our spiritual "eyes" open, glimpses of God's love will be seen each day in many forms. And our response is to give God praise for every small blessing, knowing each one is a special GIFT that we do not deserve.

"Giving thanks always for all things
to God the Father in
the name of our Lord Jesus Christ."
Ephesians 5:20

"Enter into His gates with thanksgiving,
and into His courts with praise.
Be thankful to Him, and bless His name.
For the Lord is good."
Psalm 100:4-5

The following stories remind us how God's "hugs" embrace us in our daily life through His creation around us, through other people God places in our lives, and in God's unique answers to our prayers.

We don't want to take God's gifts for granted. We thank our Lord for every blessing.

I Just Saw God

Music began. The minister, followed by the groom and best man in their tuxedos, walked up the aisle and turned toward the audience.

Bridesmaids in flowing burgundy were escorted up the aisle by groomsmen; then came the matron of honor.

The adorable Bible boy, in a tux with tails, delivered the Bible to the minister, then took his place by his mother, the matron of honor.

While almost everyone else craned their necks for that first glimpse of the bride at the rear of the wedding venue, I focused on the groom.

He stood tall, his expression somber. The music continued, then changed. The groom's countenance remained sober.

Suddenly, the groom's somber expression exploded into a smile and his whole face glowed. His eyes shone as they followed the bride, his growing smile shouting delight.

Now I knew this young man loved my niece deeply. His obvious joy strengthened my assurance that her heart was safe with him.

In that instant, I saw God.

". . . As the bridegroom rejoices over the bride,
so shall your God rejoice over you."
Isaiah 62:5

Helen Heavirland, author
My Enemy . . . My Brother
signedbytheauthor.com
College Place, Washington

Every Detail

All the while Art and I picked raspberries at a local farm, I prayed for several family members who were struggling with a health crisis and a difficult economic situation.

When we finished picking, we drove home to refrigerate the fruit. Then, we went to the grocery store to buy some Sure-Gel so I could make a batch of jam.

My daughter-in-law had told me where the Sure-Gel was located in the store, but I couldn't find it anywhere. I even asked several clerks, but none of them could help me.

I was ready to give up, when I heard the Holy Spirit say, "Just speak out loud what you're looking for."

So I did. "Lord," I said in a normal voice, "I don't know where to look for the Sure-Gel."

A woman shopping nearby turned and said kindly, "Oh honey, it's in the fourth aisle over. Look up on the third shelf. I'd be glad to take you there."

I thanked her for her help and assured her I could find it with her directions.

When I found it and reached for the box, I felt the Holy Spirit say, "I've got everything covered. I know your concerns. I understand your prayers. If I can take care of helping you find the Sure-Gel, I can care for you and your family in every way."

NOTE: God did provide help and healing for our family members. I praise and thank Him every day!

Mary (and Art) Starts
Beaverton, Oregon

One Blest Dollar

Times were tough and art sales were few. One morning I told my husband, "Next time a gallery sells one of your paintings, I need to buy a new bra. Mine is falling apart."

Our five-year-old son overheard our conversation. "Maybe you'll find one today at the garage sale, Mama," he said.

I smiled skeptically. "I don't think so, Paul."

Later, Paul handed me a dollar bill. "Here," he said proudly, holding out one of his birthday dollars with a smile. "Now you can buy a bra."

I held back tears as we got in the car. "We'll look," I said, "but I've never seen a new bra at a garage sale and I'd rather not buy another old one."

We went to several sales, buying a few ten-cent books for Paul. At the last house on our list, I spotted a stack of women's clothing on one table. On top of the pile lay a white bra.

I picked it up and saw a price tag dangling from one strap. It was brand new and had never been worn!

Paul squeezed my arm. "God put it here for you, Mama!"

"Well, I don't know. It's probably not the right size," I said.

But when I looked, there it was—the right size.

"How much is it, Mama?" Paul asked excitedly.

I'm sure you can guess: it was also the right price. On the back side of the tag, the store price was crossed out and $1.00 had been written in its place.

"My God shall supply all your needs."
Philippians 4:19

Helen Haidle, author
Journey to the Cross and Victory
Tigard, Oregon

Music in the Rain

In the span of five months, my twenty-year marriage, along with my dreams and my way of life, disintegrated. The months that followed were full of fear, anger, shock, and unbearable pain.

God kept me from despair by awakening me to the little blessings of life. Color lifted my spirits; music expressed my mood and fed my aching soul.

I learned to cherish soft textures and the smallest touch from family and friends.

One warm May evening, I opened the windows to let in the scent of lilacs and fresh mown grass. Just as I curled up in my favorite chair to read, I heard the soft patter of rain.

I glanced up to see the setting sun radiating through clouds still white with light. Incredible peace embraced me.

Soon, a new sound blended with the rain. The neighbor behind us began to strum his guitar softly on their patio. There was no particular melody, yet it was soothing and harmonious.

Tears of joy spilled down my cheeks as I laughed and praised God. Who else could have brought this all together?

My neighbor had never played his guitar on the patio before and I never heard him again.

This concert in the rain reassured me God still cared for me and loved me.

"God is love."
1 John 4:8

Beth Vice, author
Peace Within Your Borders
Tillamook, Oregon

God–Who-Finds–Things

I know from personal experience: God finds things. Once, I wrote about God helping me find our son's sweater. There have been many finds since, but my most recent is surely the best.

When my husband's hearing aids went missing, we searched for three weeks, brainstormed logical and illogical places they might be, but no-find. One day, I decided to check in his car which he'd already scoured three times.

With flashlight in hand, I got down on the cement floor of the garage and laid my head on the car floor in front of the driver's seat.

Praying to my God-Who-Finds-Things, my heart leaped when the light revealed a small black leather pouch leaning against the black runner of the car seat.

God did it again—a $5,000 find!

As I walked this morning, I was thanking the Lord anew for finding so many things over the years, when the biggest find of all occurred to me. I felt foolish for not recognizing it sooner.

God found ME! Easter 1976, God came and found me, broken and in need of a Savior. He told me about His Son, Jesus. And I believed. I praise God for the gift of salvation.

"For the Son of Man (Jesus) came to seek and to save the lost."
Luke 19:10

Donna Scales, author
My Dictionary of Praise
http://praiseposts.com
Lake Oswego, Oregon

Where's My Cat?

After my sister Sarah and I came home from school and ate a snack, Sarah started asking, "Where is the cat?"

And I said, "I don't know."

And then, my mom said, "Sarah, get the cat food and run downstairs." And she did. And my mom said to me, "Sam, help her look." And I did.

And then, we all looked everywhere in the house and still couldn't find Max. Then, my sister got the cat snacks and ran all over the place until we had no hope.

My mom and sister said, "Let's go check outside." *(We NEVER let our cat outside!)* And then we went.

Sarah sort of went down the street, but then she came back and my mom took us behind all the houses where we looked again and called for Max.

And then, when we *REALLY* had no hope, my mom prayed, "Please, Lord! Please, Lord! Please, Lord!"

Then, like three seconds later, we heard a "Meow!" and Max came out from under the deck right where we stood. Cobwebs were all over his whiskers, so I think he had fun exploring.

Mom and Sarah and I were so happy that we all cried.

God had answered our prayers! And then we went home and I hugged Max and gave him some kitty treats.

Thank You, God, for answering our prayers so quickly!

Jesus said, *"Ask, and it will be given to you; Seek, and you will find."*
Luke 11:9

Told by Sam Ifft, 6 years old
Beaverton, Oregon
3-31-2011

Snowy Dilemna

Sam, Jessica, Jed, Jay, and I laughed and told jokes as Dad drove in the Washington mountains, trying to find the perfect place to sled. I mean, what kid doesn't like sledding?

We weren't worried about anything until the car jerked to a stop. We realized we were stuck in the snow, right in the middle of a steep hill! The people in front of our van were putting chains on their tires. The problem was, we didn't have any chains!

All of us kids, except for eleven-year-old Jay, felt very scared.

Jed got upset. "Turn back!" he insisted. "I don't want to die!"

Who could blame him for crying? I would if I were eight.

So I tried to comfort Jed. "It's going to be all right," I said. "God will help us get out of this mess."

So Jed prayed, while Dad restarted the engine. But nothing happened. "God isn't answering my prayers!" exclaimed Jed.

"Sometimes, prayer takes time to be answered," I explained.

Jed frowned and looked doubtful.

Finally, Jay and his mom went outside to push the van, while Dad steered. Still, the van wouldn't budge. All of us kids fervently prayed. Suddenly, the van jerked and moved out of the rut.

Dad quickly turned the car around and headed back down the mountain to find a safer place where we could sled.

Now, Jed grinned from ear-to-ear. "Thank You, God! Thank You, God!" he repeated over and over.

"Wow!" six-year-old Jessica exclaimed. "I didn't know God could answer prayers so fast!"

Thank You Lord, for taking care of us. We are very thankful, even if You don't answer our prayers the very second we pray. I love You, God.

Sarah Ifft - age 12
Beaverton, Oregon

Was That You, God?

"What do you say we jump on the Harley and take a jaunt to our honeymoon spot?" my husband asked me one day.

"Do you think we can get enough time off work?" I responded.

Preparations made, we set out under a summer sun with blue, welcoming skies to ride 680 miles. The happy occasion of our first wedding anniversary overshadowed our heavy hearts.

"I'm sorry," the doctors had recently told me. "But you'll never be able to have children. If by chance you should become pregnant, the egg will stay in the tubes and will not be able to descend into the uterus."

These thoughts lingered as we bounced over the miles hour after hour on sometimes pot-holed roads. Only God knew what He was doing while we rode.

Finally, we reached our honeymoon motel, enjoyed our vacation days, and then headed home.

Soon after we arrived back home, I began feeling quite ill. A couple more weeks found me back in my doctor's office.

"It's a miracle pregnancy, lady!" my doctor exclaimed. "You just bounced a fertilized egg all the way down into the uterus. In eight more months, you'll be delivering a healthy baby!"

Is there any question, God, of Your providential care? What a confirmation of Your love!

Shirley Dechaine, author
Tualatin, Oregon

God's Provision

Jesus told His followers,

"Therefore I say to you,
do not worry about your life, what you will eat;
nor about the body, what you will put on.
And do not seek what you should eat or
what you should drink, nor have an anxious mind.
For all these things the nations of the world seek after,
and your Father knows that you need these things.
. . . But seek the kingdom of God,
and all these things shall be added to you.
Do not fear, little flock, for it is your Father's
good pleasure to give you the kingdom."

Luke 12:22-23, 29-32

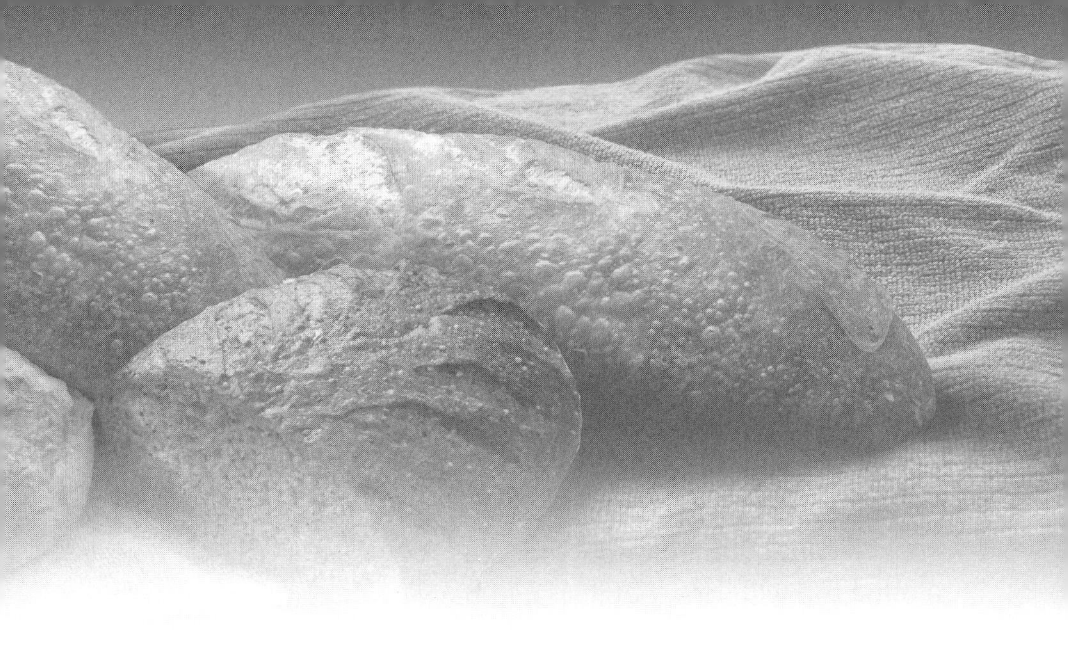

"Give us day by day our daily bread."
Luke 11:3

God's provision overflows in our everyday lives, often unnoticed. We tend to take for granted many of God's great blessings, which He freely supplies to us, even when we don't deserve them.

Each of the following stories is a reminder that our Almighty God is able to do far above what we could ask or think or even imagine!

May these testimonies from Dick, Betty, Mike, David, Elsie, Gordon and Billie increase our faith and encourage us to put God first in our lives, and then to depend on God to provide for our daily needs.

José's Rice Barrel

One day, when I arrived at the home of José, the native Choco Indian who was helping me translate the New Testament, he took me to his kitchen area and pointed excitedly to his wooden rice barrel—a six-foot wide wooden container about three feet high.

"Look!" he said. "Tell me! How did this happen?"

I stared at the barrel. Suddenly, I realized it was nearly full to the top with rice, but it should have been nearly empty. After all, the next rice crop was almost ready to be harvested.

"What's all this rice doing in your barrel?" I questioned José. "Aren't you feeding your eleven children? Isn't this the time everybody's rice starts running out? I know the planted rice hasn't been harvested."

José grinned from ear to ear. "I'm feeding my children. Here, look at my healthy sons. You can tell they aren't starving."

I was stunned. "But I remember seeing your barrel this full months ago. Why is it still so full?"

"That's what I'm asking YOU," José said. "You know that I planted less rice because I spent more time helping you translate the Bible into our native language. I thought for sure I would run out of rice some time ago."

José's wife interrupted. "And we have more to tell you! Many neighbors are asking to borrow some of our rice because they have run out. They take scoops of rice from our barrel and they've promised to pay us back when they harvest their rice in a few weeks."

José enthusiastically embraced me. "I'm thankful to God," he said. "My barrel is still full of rice, even though all the members of our family, along with many others, are eating from it. I don't understand it. Is it because I'm helping you to translate the Bible? Is it because I'm working for God?"

NOTE:

José's never-ending rice barrel was almost unbelievable. I had told José months ago to trust that God would provide for his family as he helped me translate the New Testament into Choco *(the language of the local Panamanian Indians).*

I had trusted God to provide food for José and his family so he could be my assistant, but I honestly didn't expect such an overflowing of God's goodness. I felt the Lord nudging me, "Oh, ye of little faith."

This full rice barrel became a daily witness to everyone in the village. They saw God Almighty at work in their midst, taking care of them and blessing the time and effort given by José for Bible translation work!

"[God] is able to do exceedingly abundantly above all that we ask or think, according to the power that works in us."
Ephesians 3:20

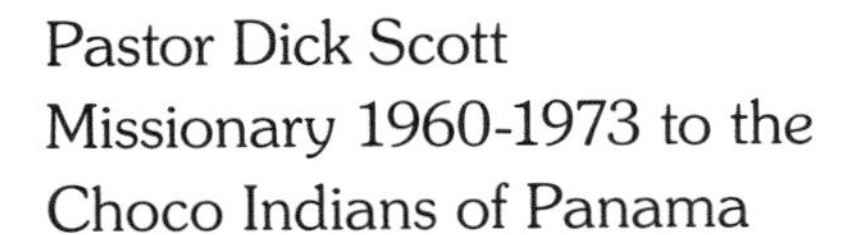

Pastor Dick Scott
Missionary 1960-1973 to the
Choco Indians of Panama

The Old Piano

About three years following my large family's move from Missouri to Southern California, we were given an old upright piano. I was ten years old, loved music, and yearned to take piano lessons. However, we were so poor we could barely afford life's necessities.

I began teaching myself, "playing" with the old piano, and before long I could play some chords, but beyond that I knew very little.

Often, I would observe others who played the piano, and I learned new things from friends and family who played, picking up pointers here and there.

Then my folks decided to move us all to Washington State when I was twelve years old. Dad bought a huge truck, piled all our belongings for the eight of us into it, and, guess what? The old piano got to come along!

Two years later, we moved back to California, along with the old heavy piano.

At age fourteen, my family began attending a small church which had no pianist. My Dad volunteered me. I could mainly play chords, but it sufficed until someone who played better came along.

Since then, music has provided me with many joyful experiences and opportunities to serve. I was a church pianist for several years. I have led a children's choir, and I have been involved in several other areas of music ministry.

More recently, I've facilitated our Beaverton Foursquare Prime Timer's Choir that has been singing together over the past ten years.

When I married my husband Loran over fifty years ago, I left the old piano behind for my younger sister to play, but most years since then I've been blessed to have a piano in my own home.

In retrospect, not only do I appreciate my parents and the old piano, but I'm grateful to the Lord for allowing me to use my limited talents for Him.

I've also seen, through the years, how God fills in a lot of the missing pieces, and as the song goes,

"Little is much when God is in it."

"Trust in the Lord with all your heart
and do not lean on your own understanding.
In all your ways acknowledge Him,
and He shall direct your paths."
Proverbs 3:5-6

Betty Trumbo
Beaverton, Oregon

Thirty-Seven Cents

"Trust Me!" Again and again, this has been God's message to me. Sometimes my test comes with big things, sometimes small, but always to strengthen my faith. For God knows we will experience the sweetness of His peace only as we completely trust Him.

Early in my journey as a Christian, my "faith tests" often involved finances. Working as a realtor, I was living inside God's workshop. Because of poor market conditions and my commission-only job, paychecks were few and far between. If I did get a sale, generally it took six to eight weeks to get paid.

So here I was again in an all too familiar position; bills were flowing in, but I had nothing in the bank or even potentially coming in to pay them.

Yes, I'd been in this same crucible of testing many times before, but somehow this time felt worse. In ten days, the bills *(about $7,700 in today's dollars)* would come due. Owing a million dollars would have felt no worse to me. I was at a crossroads in a seemingly impossible situation.

As a young dad with a stay-at-home wife, I was working at least seventy-five hours a week, mostly out of fear and my deep sense of responsibility for my family. I was exhausted, frustrated, and broke . . . or so I thought. I had only thirty-seven cents.

But after shedding more than a few "unmanly" tears, my countenance brightened as what felt like a brainstorm washed over me. "No, I wasn't broke. I still had thirty-seven cents!"

So, with the support of my wife, we decided to *blow* most of our fortune on a pack of gum; twenty-five cents!

With a remaining net worth of twelve cents, I was free to declare to my wife *(and in the Lord's earshot)*, "Now we are broke! Now God has to do something!"

You're probably thinking there must be a great ending to this story, because otherwise this author would be dead by starvation. Yes, the Lord did come through, with flying colors!

But, no matter how hard I try, I cannot remember how the Lord met our need. What I do remember, however, is that on the day our bills were due, not only did we have the money to pay all of our bills, we had about $200 in surplus.

Reflecting back on this particular miracle *(one of many thousands in my life),* I smile as I remember the extra that was "left over." Just as when Jesus fed the crowd of 5,000, He still supplies above and beyond what is needed or required.

I wish I could say I've learned this lesson of God's provision so well that I'll never be anxious about finances again.

But I can tell you that my seasons of financial testing are much more manageable now because I know for certain—in my mind, heart, and experientially—that God is faithful and good all the time!

Be encouraged with me: God is fully worthy of all our trust!

"If we are faithless, [God] will remain faithful, for He cannot disown himself."
2 Timothy 2:13 NIV

Pastor Mike Kinsman
Encore Ministries
Beaverton Foursquare Church
Beaverton, Oregon

Faith . . . in Spite of Circumstances

In 1977 my wife and I searched in vain for a house to buy. With three preschoolers, we needed a house on a quiet street, hopefully with sidewalks and a park nearby. I needed space for my art studio. It was difficult finding all of this in an inexpensive home. And we discovered very quickly that no bank wanted to lend money to a struggling, free-lance artist.

One rainy November day, Helen and I bundled our three preschoolers into the car and drove to Beaverton to look at a new housing development. At this point in our search, we needed to find a builder who was willing to sell us a house on a contract.

After a discouraging talk with the development builders, we trudged silently back to the car, buckled in our kids, and headed home. Gloom hung over us like the thick fog which covered our city.

Suddenly from the back seat, our daughter who had just turned three years old began to sing in a soft, sweet voice:

"Holy Ghost, what a wonder You are.
Holy Ghost, what a wonder You are.
You lead us. You guide us. You live right inside us.
Holy Ghost, what a wonder You are."

Helen reached over and squeezed my arm. "Is God speaking to us?" she whispered. "'Out of the mouth of babes . . . .' Let's trust the Lord WILL guide us."

The words of the song brought new encouragement from the Lord. Our hope was reignited. Our gloom lifted. We knew God was strengthening our faith. Somehow, somewhere, and in some way, God would lead us to a home of our own.

Shortly after this, our realtor Mike Kinsman found us a builder who sold us a house on a one–year contract.

In faith, we signed the contract and moved into the house, not knowing whether we would have enough art sales by the end of twelve months to be eligible for an Oregon GI loan.

During the next eight months, only two of my paintings sold. We prayed, trusting God to work something out.

Then, nine months after we moved into the house, there was a rash of sales as the Portland Art Association selected me as the recipient of their support for local artists.

During the next two months, God worked a miracle! Just exactly the "right" number of paintings sold to qualify me for an Oregon GI loan.

NOTE: Ironically, after signing the loan, there was not one sale of my art work during the next four months! But this only reinforced Helen's and my faith that God will provide ***what*** we need, ***when*** we need it.

*"I am the Lord your God,
Who leads you by the
way you should go."*
Isaiah 48:17

David Haidle
Painter & Illustrator
Portland, Oregon

Above & Beyond

"Mom," my eldest daughter said as she was leaving for middle school, "I don't have time to pack for the retreat. Mrs. Osgood is picking me up at four o'clock. The list is on my bed. Will you pack my bag?"

Even though I had more than I could do that day, I said I would.

After the older girls were off to school and the two little ones cared for, I took time to look at the list.

Oh, NO. The list of clothing items included a dress for a formal dinner.

What was I going to do? I could probably sew something, but I could never get it finished in one day.

At this time, I was in the middle of a divorce. I was a working mom of five daughters from the ages of three to twelve years old, and I was broke. What could I possibly do?

I started ironing, dampening the dresses with my tears and telling God just how bad things were turning out.

Just then a car pulled into my driveway and "Emma" got out. I had hired her as a baby sitter a couple of years ago, but my kids couldn't stand her and she didn't like me, so she had quit in a huff.

Emma was an older woman who always set out on a mission to "get this family organized."

It turned out that Emma had been hired to organize closets for a wealthy family and now she had a box of clothes they were giving away. She asked me if I wanted the assortment of clothing. I didn't want to hurt her feelings, so I said yes.

When she left, I opened the box, feeling defeated.

To my amazement, on top of the pile of blouses, skirts, and tee-shirts, lay a formal gown carefully wrapped in white tissue paper. I realized it was the right size for my daughter and knew it would fit her perfectly!

God had heard my cry for help.

I thought about how God had helped us various times in the past, but now I knew that HE was the husband and father we could always count on.

Matthew 6:28-30 says that we are not to worry about what we will wear because God knows what we need. Even King Solomon in all his glory was not adorned as beautifully as the lilies of the field.

Now, God had graciously clothed my daughter in the most beautiful gown I had ever seen. Praise HIM!

"Now to Him who is able to do
exceedingly abundantly above
all that we ask or think . . .
to Him be glory in the church by Christ Jesus
to all generations, forever and ever. Amen."
Ephesians 3:20-21

Elsie Heuerman
Vancouver, Washington

Radical Change

At the age of fourteen, my dad was an alcoholic. At six foot two, weighing 256 pounds, people called him "Old Killer Prunt."

Glen, my dad, worked at the Portland shipyards and Billie, my mother, was a cocktail waitress. She also was an alcoholic.

I remember one night they came home late, screaming and fighting. I looked out of my room just in time to see my mom throw a butcher knife at my dad. It cut through the waves in his hair and stuck in the kitchen wall.

One day our neighbor, (5'6" and 130 pounds) knocked on our door and asked, "Mr. Prunty, would you like to go to Sunday School with me?"

Dad cussed him out, but this neighbor kept coming over and wouldn't give up. Finally, Dad decided to set a five-gallon pail filled with water beside the front door.

The next time Mr. Beyers came to invite Dad to go to church, my father dumped the whole bucket over him, drenching his three-piece suit and the Bible he held.

But on Wednesday night, Mr. Beyers came back again! And my dad went to prayer service with him. That night, Dad's life changed drastically. He received the Lord as his personal Savior.

Mom still went out with her girlfriends and came home drunk. But Dad always cleaned her up and put her in bed. Then, he would kneel down beside her bed and pray for her.

A year later, when Mom finally came to the Lord, all her bad habits were gone, just like that. I saw God transform my parents from alcoholics into missionaries!

Gordon Prunty
Son of Rev. Glen and Billie Prunty
Beaverton, Oregon

Needing God's Care

When my husband and I served as missionaries in Venezuela, our two children attended boarding school in Bogota, Columbia. They came to live with us during their grade school vacations.

One summer, Glenda and Gordon had been with us for only a couple of days when a dangerous situation arose.

I had taken Glenda to the outhouse we'd built in back of our grass hut. (She had beautiful, long, dark hair and we never let her go anywhere alone because of the danger of her being stolen by the natives.)

While we were out there, my husband called loudly, "Billie! Lock the toilet door! Stay there until I come to get you!"

We waited until finally Glen knocked on the door. When I opened it, he was standing there with two suitcases in his hands. "Get in the boat right now," he said. "I'll explain later."

Obediently, we followed him and our son down to the river, and soon we were paddling our boat to a nearby town.

During the boat trip, Glen explained what had happened. "The Indian village chief came to our door and he announced to me, 'I want to court your daughter. I want her for a wife.'"

We had heard of more than one case where Indians killed whoever stood in their way in choosing a wife. Glen knew the chief wouldn't accept a "no" from us as parents.

So we stayed in a little apartment in town until our children's school break was over and they could return to their studies. We prayed for them continually, always entrusting them to God's care.

Billie Prunty Hawkins, missionary
Choco Indian Missions, Panama
King City, Oregon

Unseen Power

It was a long journey to our boarding school in Columbia. First, we got on a cargo plane with no seats. My sister and I were sitting on sacks of rice and beans when, suddenly, the plane rolled and dipped. Finally, the copilot came back to get us, and he strapped us in with him and the pilot up in the cockpit.

When we landed in a little airport, we got to look at the belly of the plane—it had been riddled with bullets!

The pilots got us transferred to a pick-up truck to take us the rest of the trip over the mountain. The treacherous, one-lane road was lined with cliffs and chasms on both sides of the road.

Whenever we came to a curve on the hillside, the driver would honk the horn loudly to find out if anyone was coming from the other side.

As our driver drove around one bend in the road, I looked out the side window. I was surprised to see a deeply-cut chasm, cascading about 1,000 feet below the road we were on.

After a long, harrowing drive, we finally arrived at our school for missionary children.

One week later, a taxicab driver drove up to our school. He asked, "Did an American boy and a girl with long, black hair arrive here last week? I'd like to talk to them."

He explained why he was looking for us. "Some people hired me to drive them out of the area where the civil war had broken out. As I drove up the mountain, I was following a pickup truck with two American children in it.

"The truck driver slowed down when he came to one very dangerous bend in the road. He honked, then continued around the corner. But as I watched, I only saw the *left* tires on the driver's side of the truck touch the washed-out road.

"The tires on the passenger side floated in mid-air. It looked like someone had placed a big sheet of glass under the tires."

"I stopped my car and walked over to see if I could drive across that part of the road with my smaller car. But there was only two feet of road left there. The rest of the roadway had broken off, leaving a great chasm of about 1,000 feet down the cliff. I had to back up my taxi to a wider section of road, turn around, and drive back down the mountain. I guessed that the children were being delivered to this school, so I drove the long way around the mountain in order to reach your school."

One of the school teachers brought my sister and me to meet the taxi driver. He shared his story and then said, "I came to find out what kind of special powers you children have."

Glenda and I told him, "*We* don't have any special powers. It was God our heavenly Father who saved our lives."

Baffled, he wouldn't believe us. He left, shaking his head.

All of this reminded my sister and me that God intervenes in our lives, even when we don't know what is going on.

"Underneath are the everlasting arms."
Deuteronomy 33:27

Gordon Prunty
Beaverton, Oregon

Sending out Ripples

Throughout the Old and New Testament, we read about the Almighty God who works in people's hearts and lives during painful struggles, in the midst of valleys, in times of sorrow and tragedy, and even in death.

It's a gift from God to be able to see His hand in every situation, knowing He is the great Redeemer who can redeem all wrongs, even our own mistakes and failures.

As we celebrate what God has done in each other's lives, we can even celebrate challenging times, because our God is teaching us, growing us, and maturing us.

God IS ABLE to deliver, but even if He does NOT do what I expect or ask, I can still trust His love and faithfulness.

The one and only thing that counts is God's love for us. And nothing, absolutely nothing, can change that reality.

"Consider it pure joy, my brothers,
whenever you face trials of many kinds,
because you know that the testing of your faith
develops perseverance.
Perseverance must finish its work so that
you may be mature and complete, not lacking anything."
James 1:2-4 NIV

Let the stories in this section by Shirley, Dannah, Tito, Kristy, Helen, and Jay encourage your heart to firmly trust the Lord and to be ready to move as He leads. Our lives do make a difference to others.

God wants to work in and through all of us as we impact those around us with "ripples" of His life.

Itty-bitty Bouquets

Because of a traumatic brain injury I suffered from an auto accident, I was forced to move into a retirement center early. I am the youngest person living here—the "baby." I did not want to move into this place, but the Lord guided me very strongly to come. So I obeyed.

When I settled into the corner unit, I realized that the area outside was hard, bare ground. There was no way I could grow anything.

But I didn't know how I would be able to live if I couldn't plant any flowers. Sweet peas, especially, have been such an important part of my life. I use them in many of my paintings and I also draw colorful sweet peas on the gift cards I make.

So in prayer, I asked the Lord what I should do.

Now I'm gardening and planting in all kinds of containers and hanging pots. My boxes and pots filled with sweet peas, roses, daisies, and many herbs attract other residents to my corner apartment.

One blind lady walks by my corner unit every day. I give her a fragrant flower like a sweet pea, or a feathery peppermint or thyme leaf to touch and smell.

People in the assisted living section of this retirement center can't come outside to see my garden, so I go to them.

A lot of them are forgotten or their families are too busy to come.

But they still need someone to talk to, someone who will listen, and someone to pray with them.

So I bring them gifts of pink and purple sweet peas in little vases.

When I run out of vases, I wrap old prescription bottles in colorful tissue paper. I've discovered that everybody loves an itty-bitty bouquet to brighten their room.

I bring special gifts of sweet peas and daisies to the deathbeds of my fellow residents. When I place the tiny bouquets by a bedside, it touches the family of the person who is dying.

My sweet peas and flowers bring back people's memories of joy in a back yard, a garden, or a hillside where they used to play as a child.

The flowers' fragrances also bless people by bringing back sweet memories to those who are now losing their memories as well as their physical abilities.

(Continued on next page)

Shirley Embanks

"Itty-Bitty Bouquets" continued . . .

I didn't want to move to this retirement center, but now I thank God for the privilege of giving the simple gift of a flower to many residents who have become my friends. How it warms my heart. It's been such a special joy to share my sweet peas—a fragrance of Christ—and to pray with others.

I like to encourage people, "If all you can do is pour a cup of tea, then pour a cup of tea. If all you can do is give one sweet pea, then give one!"

Jesus said, *"Inasmuch as you did it to one of the least of these My brethren, you did it to Me."*
Matthew 25:40

Shirley Embanks
Portland, Oregon

Touched by God

I have wrestled professionally all over the country, with many well-known wrestlers. In my long career as a "macho man" wrestler, I lived apart from my wife quite a while.

When I finally quit wrestling and returned home to my family, I took up art, which I'd done a lot, even as a kid, and I began sign painting for various stores in the Northwest.

I ended up as head of the art and sign department for Payless. After work, I would go out and have a drink with the guys, then return home pretty high.

It was hard on my wife. She was watching Billy Graham at this time and she told me, "Tito, you have to charge your life."

"Don't tell me what to do!" I responded angrily. I considered myself a member of a church, but I didn't know God in a personal way.

One month, my son and I took a crew to paint and fix up the Payless Drug store in Redding, California. The first night, I went into a drug store and bought several six packs of beer.

The pharmacist manager of the drug store came over to me and asked, "Tito, why don't you go to church with me?"

Well, I looked at him, looked at my beer, and grinned.

"Go to church with me this Sunday," he urged. "Here's my phone number. I'll come pick you up at ten o'clock."

But on Saturday evening neither my son nor I wanted to go to church the next day, so I phoned and told him, "I can't make it tomorrow." On the second and third Saturdays, I phoned and cancelled out again.

On our last weekend in Redding, I went to call him again, but I couldn't find his phone number. I looked everywhere, but I never found the paper on which I'd written his number.

I was so mad! Now I knew he would come pick me up. I was being *forced* to go to church with him!

Sunday morning he came and drove me to church. He went to sit in the front with his family, but I insisted on sitting in the last chair in the last row. I wanted to be able to get out fast.

The sermon was okay, so I didn't get up and leave.

At the end, the pastor asked everyone to stand up. He said we should raise our hands to God and pray. So I stood up and I raised my hands, too.

But when I looked up, I suddenly found myself praying, "God, I can't change my life. You have to help me. Please God, take the devil out of my heart."

When I finished and lowered my hands, the peace of God powerfully swept over me. (Today I still am brought to tears just remembering it.)

My friend found me after the service and saw me weeping. He asked, "Do you want to change your life and receive Christ?"

I could hardly speak. "Yes. . . yes . . . ," I said tearfully.

"What in your life bothers you the most?" he asked.

I felt devastated as I told him, "I'm ruining my home and my family by my actions." More tears followed with much prayer.

When my friend finally drove me back to the Payless store where my son was working, I got another surprise.

As soon as my son saw me, he took me aside.

"Dad," he said, "I have to talk to you. I know that something happened to you today in church, because at one point when I stood up here in the store, I felt a wave of peace come over me so strong, I knew it had to be God!"

"Whoa!" I was shocked to know God was working in my son's life as well as in mine!

My whole life changed completely, and so did the lives of

those in my family. I quit drinking *cold turkey*.

Shortly afterwards, I also quit smoking and I threw out all my cigars. But when I went to throw away my last book of matches, I hesitated for some unknown reason.

Opening the matchbook flap, I saw something white stuck inside. Reaching for it, I found a small piece of neatly folded paper tucked in behind the few remaining matches.

When I unfolded the paper, I saw a number written on it. At first I didn't know what the number was or where I got it.

Finally, I realized—this was the phone number I couldn't find that last Saturday when I tried to call the manager and get out of going to church!

I looked up towards heaven and smiled.

"God," I said, "You did that, didn't You?"

"If anyone is in Christ, he is a new creation;
old things have passed away;
. . . all things have become new."

2 Corinthians 5:17

Tito Carreon
Beaverton, Oregon

For God's Purposes

Just before my fiftieth birthday, for the first time in my life, I was totally alone. My grown children were attending colleges in different states. My marriage of thirty plus years was in the final stages of disintegration.

I did not know what the future held for me. I did know I was experiencing the deepest grief I'd ever experienced.

Not even the death of my baby daughter had prepared me for these feelings of isolation, guilt and shame.

Co-workers gave me the Jeremiah scripture—*The Lord has a plan for you, to prosper you. . .* But still, what kind of a future can a fifty-year-old woman have?

Then, two ladies twenty years my senior befriended me. They had already walked this same path, yet they had survived, and each of their lives was full to overflowing.

To my great surprise and amazement, I thrived!

I was able to take a trip to the Holy Lands and later I joined a mission team that served in Kazakstan. I also began to pursue the passion God placed deep in my heart.

The deep grief of divorce I walked through has been felt by nearly one-half of the population in the USA. And now the Lord lets me encourage others, just as those two dear ladies encouraged me.

"I'll show up and take care of you as I promised . . . I have it all planned out—plans to take care of you, not abandon you, plans to give you the future you hope for."
Jeremiah 29:11 (The Message)

Dannah Taylor
Beaverton, Oregon

New Assignment

One evening, my mother phoned from her home in Iowa. "My bad knee keeps me home-bound, but God showed me something special I can do for you every day. In fact, *three* times a day," she said excitedly. "I'll pray like Daniel—morning, noon, and night. I've made a commitment to pray for all of you three times each day." *(See Daniel 6:10)*

Until she died five years later, my mother faithfully continued her "Daniel prayers." She felt it was her assignment from God.

When she awoke each morning, she praised God, then prayed specific prayers for each child and grandchild. She prayed for her eight siblings, along with all their children and grandchildren.

After lunch, our beloved "Oma" would read her worn Bible and pray once more. At night, she took time to pray again.

"I'm praying down three generations," she explained to me. "My mother prayed for her children, her grandchildren, and her great grandchildren. I'm doing the same. I hope you will, too," she added. "Remember how Lois handed her faith down to her daughter Eunice and to Timothy, her grandson." *(2 Timothy 1:5)*

Many other people in Iowa City and Mt. Vernon also valued Oma's daily prayers. As we hugged one another on the day of her funeral, we asked each other, "Who will pray for us now?"

Leaving the cemetery, a new thought filled me with comfort and hope: **"Her prayers still surround you and will continue to bless you."**

"Pray without ceasing."
1 Thessalonians 5:17

Ella "Oma" Beckman
by Helen Beckman Haidle

From Fear to Joy

If you had told me three years ago that I would be ministering in a detention center today, I would not have believed you.

However, while reading in our church bulletin about a ministry called Rosemont, I was surprised by the instant connection the Holy Spirit placed in my heart.

It was a calling that would not leave me; so finally I said, "Yes, God. I will obey you."

Rosemont is a secured state treatment center and school in Portland, Oregon, for girls thirteen to eighteen years of age. I remember feeling nervous and unsure of how I could relate to these girls.

Then I remembered my own rebellion as a teenager and my darkest hour of losing a baby at the age of seventeen.

Shortly after this difficult time in my teens, I had surrendered my life to God and He gave me a desire to study and obey His Word.

I realized I could give the girls at Rosemont His powerful Word that heals and restores, like it is still doing for me today!

God continues to give me a double blessing through obeying His call.

When I talk to the girls about God's unfailing love, God reminds me of His sacrifice for me.

As I prepare a talk about forgiveness, God convicts me to forgive those who have hurt or wronged me.

As I share with the girls about the Holy Spirit's work in our lives, He comforts my own soul.

As I pray over the girls' prayer requests, which they write in our special prayer notebook, I am able to lay my own burdens at the cross.

When I send a birthday card to one girl or when I celebrate Christmas with all the girls, it brings joy to my heart.

After I write the girls to encourage them, I am energized.

When I lead them in worship, I know God works miracles!

God has taken away the spirit of fear I once had, and has blessed me with a boldness to share His mercy as well the reality of His judgment.

Many of these girls have been abused and neglected. I'm thrilled to receive hugs from them as they begin to open up and trust my love for them.

Most of all, I am thankful to God for bringing them hope and peace when they say, "Yes" to Him.

It is an honor to love these girls and to work alongside a team of brothers and sisters in Christ who have welcomed me into this ministry.

I'm so glad I said "Yes" to God's calling.

"He guides me along right paths
to bring honor to His Name."
Psalm 23:3 NLT

Kristy Benz
Tigard, Oregon

Even if God Doesn't . . .

I have never forgotten the Sunday in 1983 when Pastor Ron Mehl came out just before the worship began and announced, "Dell Ferguson died early this morning. Even though we prayed continually for Dell's healing, the Lord chose to take him to his heavenly home. In the midst of their loss, Dell's family is standing like the three friends who faced the fiery furnance. His wife Deanie wanted me to tell all of you that she trusts God like Shadrach, Meshach, and AbedNego who said, 'Our God is able to deliver us, but **even if He doesn't,** we will still not lose faith or deny Him.'"

At this time I felt a great disappointment with God in my own life. This family's faith was a reminder to me that, when God does NOT do what I ask and believe for, I can still trust Him.

I can face failure, death, or the death of my loved one with confidence that "God is able." By faith I *am able* to trust God's answer to my prayers. No matter what the answer is, I can be sure God loves me.

"Our God whom we serve is able
to deliver us from the burning fiery furnace,
and He will deliver us from your hand, O king.
But if not, *let it be known to you, O king, that we will not...*
worship the gold image which you have set up."

Daniel 3:17-18

Dell & Deanie Ferguson
& Family - *photo taken in 1980*
Portland, Oregon
(by Helen Haidle)

No Thanks!

Twenty years ago, after an out-of-town business meeting, a group of us met for a relaxing dinner and conversation. Then alcohol was served to the group, but I didn't want any.

Drinking was something I just didn't do.

After the meeting, my managers criticized me for being a wet blanket on the gathering that evening. And in the weeks following, they taught me how to be a social drinker.

Drinking then became something I did. But that was the beginning; let's fast-forward to the end of the story.

Twenty years now past, I attended a two-day sales meeting in an Atlanta hotel. The waiter who came to take drink orders, started where the head manager and I were sitting.

My boss ordered a drink, but I told the waiter, "No, thanks."

You see, after years of saying "Yes", I had learned it was far better to say "No." Saying "Yes" had brought me much trouble, including a failed marriage.

The younger men across the table from me quickly followed suit, and also said, "No thanks."

The "no"s continued down the entire long narrow table.

This is the first time I ever heard so many "no's" on such an occasion. I knew my choice had empowered the other young men to abstain, even after our boss said "Yes," and the Lord used this experience to strengthen my testimony.

"Let your light so shine before men, that they may see your good works and glorify your Father in heaven."
Matthew 5:16

Jay Snell
Beaverton, Oregon

Precious Good-byes

Jesus said,
"I am the resurrection and the life. He who believes in Me, though he may die, he shall live. And whoever lives and believes in Me shall never die. Do you believe this?"
John 11:25-26

Sometimes a life ends quickly and unexpectedly.

At other times, there are opportunities given to say good-bye.

None of us knows exactly what would be best for us and for the others involved.

Only God sees the whole picture. So we can trust even the END of our life—and the end of our loved ones' lives—to the Lord, knowing how much He cares for each one of us.

"And God will wipe away
every tear from their eyes;
there shall be no more death,
nor sorrow, nor crying;
and there shall be no more pain,
for the former things have passed away."
Revelation 21:4

The following individuals have been willing to share some of their deepest feelings and thoughts regarding the departure of a loved one, whether it is an infant, a parent, a brother, a first-born child, or a marriage partner of many years.

Every incident touches every one of us because the Lord has told us to share one another's sorrows as well as joys.

As you read these tender accounts, thank the Lord for His faithfulness to comfort and carry these families as well as carry each of us through the sorrow and heartaches that accompany the death of someone we cherish.

Time of Trust

My husband and I were thankful to be part of Bill and Marian vanBaggen's home fellowship group. Their warm, welcoming spirits made the group such a joy to attend.

At the end of one of our home group meetings, Marian walked to the door with me. While I put on my coat, she explained the test results of her last doctor's visit.

"It's such a rare disease I have," she said. "The doctors told me there is no cure for it, but now they're giving me some new medications which they hope will slow its progression."

Seeing the concerned look on my face, she quickly added, "I know everything is going to be alright. I'm in God's hands, and isn't that a good place to be?"

I smiled and agreed as I hugged her, but my heart ached at the prospect of losing a special friend. Her health situation sounded very grim.

Marian went on to share. "Yesterday, at the Wednesday prayer service, the pastor asked us to do something special. He suggested we would quietly wait for a word from the Lord and see what God would place in our heart and mind." Her face glowed as she retold this to me.

"As I waited before the Lord," she said, "immediately the word 'TRUST' came to me. I felt the Lord urge me to completely trust Him with my heart condition. So I'm not going to worry about anything. It's in the Lord's hands."

Walking out the front door, I felt so uplifted by Marian's attitude of faith amid dire health circumstances.

Two weeks later, David and I visited Marian in the hospital. None of us knew she had only three days left to live. Once again, Marian's faith and trust in the Lord gave her strength.

"I'm taking a day at a time," she said. "I know God's timing in everything will be just perfect. He has to work out every detail. And God alone knows the best timing, because this doesn't just involve me; it involves everyone else in our family."

Marian's eyes sparkled as she spoke of her husband.

"In all of my health issues, Bill has helped in every way possible. I'm so proud of him. He gets ready for our home study group and cleans up afterwards. And he assists me whenever I need it."

David and I agreed—Bill was a very special man!

Before we left, the three of us joined hands and prayed. There was such peace in that room. I silently thanked the Lord for the friendship of this special woman, and for letting me see her example of perfect peace in the midst of knowing she may not have long to live.

Marian faced the future with full confidence, knowing she was in God's loving hands. She was determined to TRUST her Lord to the end—which she did.

"Yea, though I walk through the valley of the shadow of death, I will fear no evil, for Thou art with me."
Psalm 23:4 KJV

In honor of Marian vanBaggen
Entered Heaven March 2010
(by Helen Haidle)

Holding Hands

Bob Reed told his wife, "I'm going to beat this cancer." He did everything he could, but chemotherapy reacted badly in his body and his physical condition worsened.

We all know Dad as the life of the party—smiling, cracking jokes, making everyone feel important. Now he lies in bed very lifeless. It is a cold reality.

August 16th, 2007.

This last week for me has been a very busy week. I have been traveling a lot for work. I have really missed him this last week, especially during a season in which it has been the hardest for both my dad and my mom.

So tonight I decided to go over and see him. Since last Friday my father has been bedridden.

Think of that: *Bob Reed bedridden.* It just doesn't fit.

As I drove the lonely road over to my parents' house, I kept trying to imagine what it would be like to see my dad in this state. Nothing could prepare me for what I saw. Dad was very frail and skinny. His skin was white, and he looked cold and weak.

So I hopped into bed next to him and just lay there without saying a word.

He said quietly, "Hi, Joe."

I said hi back.

We laid there for the next ten minutes, not saying anything more. Then my dad did something powerful. He reached out from under the covers to hold my hand.

It was the first time I could ever recall holding hands with my father. I am sure we probably did it when I was a kid, but now, as adults, we were loving each other the best way we knew how.

Holding hands with my father reminded me of a thought that Phillip Yancey, author of *Where Is God When It Hurts?*, shared in his book. He said that, when people hurt, God is there in those people who reach out to care for one another.

God was with us tonight and God has been with my family in so many ways through many people who reach out to care.

Holding hands. It is a simple thing, but it can mean so much. We're thankful for everyone who held hands with us through this process.

This has been a hard season for us, but we understand that God is good during the hardest of times. We have had great support from family and friends that sustained our every step. Our final time together has been very sweet.

"Rejoice with those who rejoice,
and weep with those who weep."
Romans 12:15

Joseph & Amy (Reetz) Reed, Lewis & Leonard
Portland, Oregon

From Death to Life

I stood outside a patient's room and nervously watched the middle-aged man motion frantically to the nurse for his suction tube. He had no jaw, and across his shoulders were open and oozing sores. I could see fear and desperation in his eyes.

I prayed silently, *"Oh Lord. Please. Not this man."*

As a young nurses' aide, I felt inadequate to care for him. But Mr. Anderson did become my patient, and God's Spirit urged me to share His eternal hope found in the Bible.

I resisted and made excuses. But I had no peace until I finally prayed, "Lord, I'm willing; help me."

My opportunity came that night. I stood at the foot of Mr. Anderson's bed, looked into his eyes and said, "I'm a Christian. May I tell you God's good news?"

He sat up, fixed his eyes on me, and nodded, "Yes."

I smiled and said, "God loves you. Jesus died for your sins, was buried, and rose again." I ended with John 3:16. *"For God so loved the world that He gave His only begotten Son, that whoso-ever believes in Him should not perish, but have everlasting life."*

Then I asked him the important question I knew would change his life forever. "Mr. Anderson," I said quietly, "would you like to ask Jesus to be your Lord and Savior?"

He nodded yes, grabbed my hands and closed his eyes to pray. After I prayed, I opened my eyes and saw tears streaming down his face. He gratefully shook my hands.

The next day, Mr. Anderson took a nap at noon, and he woke up in the presence of His Savior.

Geraldine "Jerry" Buss, author
Salem, Oregon

Mysterious Ways

I remember the first time I met Kenny. He came to the house to meet with my husband, Troy. When I answered the door, there stood a thirty-six-year-old man with brown eyes and a warm smile. I liked him instantly.

The time the three of us shared that afternoon is one I will never forget. As we talked and laughed together, there were some emotional moments too.

Kenny asked us about our marriage, and what advice we might share. "I want what the two of you have," he said, as his eyes filled with tears.

Kenny had never married, but he still hoped he would find the right person and experience the love he saw between us.

What was so poignant in this discussion was the fact that Kenny knew his life was going to be cut short. He had been diagnosed with Lou Gehrig's disease, a fatal and cruel disease, which would most likely end his life in the next two years.

My husband Troy had the same disease. It had already ravaged his body and left ninety percent of his muscles useless and atrophied.

Kenny's purpose in coming to our house was to meet Troy and learn more about the disease and how to prepare for it.

But God had a different purpose. What Kenny experienced instead was the presence of God in our lives. Now, he wanted "what we had." Even though Kenny didn't recognize that or share our Christian faith, we said we would be praying for him.

After Troy died, I visited Kenny at his parents' home. At this time, the disease had started to take its toll, and he needed a wheelchair to get around.

As Kenny introduced me to Melanie, his caregiver, I saw a twinkle in his eye. Then, the two of them announced to me that they were married . . . and expecting a baby!

 (Continued on next page)

I felt overjoyed to see Kenny have his dream come true, yet I grieved, knowing the difficult road that lay ahead for them.

It was heart wrenching that Troy wasn't there to share the good news, but he had gone to be with the Lord a few months earlier. Yet I knew it was Troy's heart, as well as mine, to share with Kenny the love and hope of Jesus.

Months later, I was shocked to receive a phone call from Kenny's mother who told me Kenny had moved back to their house after he and Melanie separated. She asked me to come and visit. I assured her I would.

All the way there, I prayed about what I could say. I had thought God had given Kenny some happiness on this earth in the midst of a horrendous disease. Now, how could this be God's plan?

On my way out the door I had grabbed a copy of Pastor Ron Mehl's book, *Meeting God at a Dead End.* I couldn't imagine how things could be more hopeless for Kenny than they were at this point. He needed God more than ever, yet he continued to look for Him in the wrong places.

Whenever I asked Kenny about God, he always said, "Yes, I believe in God." But I knew he was missing the personal relationship and saving grace of surrendering his life to Jesus Christ.

Sitting at his bedside and crying together, I held Kenny's hand and promised to return soon. I left the book and he gave a half-hearted promise to have his night nurse read it to him.

The next week I returned to visit and noticed the book on his night stand. Before I had a chance to ask, he shared that a hospice volunteer was reading it to him and he was enjoying it.

I knew the seeds of hope were starting to grow. I also knew time was growing short for Kenny. I silently prayed for the words and the courage to share the message of salvation.

"Kenny," I said, "remember when you told us you wanted what Troy and I had?"

Kenny's smile lit up as he slowly nodded his head. By now words were difficult to form. His speech was severely impaired by the loss of his tongue and throat muscles. He sounded just like Troy did before his speech was entirely gone. I had to fight the strong emotions that welled up inside of me.

I shared that having Jesus at the center of our marriage was the reason for the strong relationship Troy and I had. And without Jesus, I didn't have any idea how we could have withstood the challenges of life, let alone the added strain of the illness.

I shared with Kenny the prayers Troy and I prayed for him. I talked about heaven and how Troy wanted him there one day.

With tears rolling down his face, Kenny agreed that he wanted to know Jesus in this way, too.

Together we prayed as Kenny surrendered his life to the Lord. Joy and peace flooded the room where there had been such hopelessness.

The ways of God are such a mystery. A tragic illness brought Kenny and Troy together in this life. In God's great mercy, He used this to accomplish His goal of drawing Kenny to Himself and into eternal life. And, in the final weeks of his life, Kenny and Melanie came back together as a family, united in the Lord with new love for one another.

"All things work together for good for those who love God, who are called according to His purpose."
Romans 8:28

Marilyn Thompson
"Victoria's Lavender"
Newberg, Oregon

Who's in "Control"

My younger siblings used to call me "The Controller."

That's who I was, out of choice and out of necessity. My alcoholic dad and very ill mom meant life was out of control. The responsibility of maintaining our home and helping three younger siblings fell on my shoulders.

At age sixteen, I took control of my own life and jumped into a marriage in order to escape living at home. But I married an alcoholic. My poor choice! That marriage ended after eight years and one child.

Still *in control,* I married another alcoholic. After many years of a second difficult marriage, God intervened and touched my heart as I attended meetings at Al-Anon *(a special group for friends and families of problem drinkers).*

It was through Al-Anon & Alcoholics Anonymous that John and I learned we could give full control of our lives to God. We also learned that the Lord is a redeeming and faithful God.

Sobriety and sanity returned to our home as we and our sons grew in faith and relationship with Jesus.

In October 1992, we decided to sign up for a 1993 spring trip to Israel with Pastor Ron and other Beaverton Foursquare members. Every week we attended the planning meetings and our excitement grew. We finally saved enough money for the trip down payment, which was due in January.

But, halfway through December, John sat me down one evening.

"Honey," he said, "I know you're going to be really upset, but we are not going to Israel. I know the Lord is telling us not to go."

UPSET was not an adequate word for how I felt and how I reacted!

But when I calmed down, I knew that, if John had heard from the Lord, there was no bucking it. After all, we had given God complete control over our lives. He would lead us. So I finally yielded my will to His.

On January 1, 1993, John retired and he then began work on remodeling our home. Pastor Ron and the tour group from our church left for Israel without us on March 8th.

The next day, on March 9th, when I arrived home from work, John was eager to show me the remodeling jobs he and our son had accomplished that day.

As John stood at the kitchen counter talking to me about his plans for the new remodel, he suddenly collapsed and fell to the floor.

I immediately called 911. When the ambulance arrived, paramedics rushed John to the nearest hospital.

Soon, all of my children, along with Pastor Chuck, joined me at the hospital. God graciously provided much emotional support for the moment when the doctors came and told us that John had died.

Later, when I reflected on this, I saw how God had so mercifully timed it all. To this day, God—my constant and faithful companion—is still in ***control*** of my life.

"God Himself has promised,
'I will never leave you
nor forsake you.'"
Hebrews 13:5

Bonnie Mercer
Compassion First Ministry
Grief-Share Ministry
Beaverton, Oregon

My Tiny Tim

On October 8, 2008, our family of six learned we would be a family of seven. The news was rather overwhelming and quite a shock to everyone. Our children's ages were five, seven, twelve, and fourteen. I was forty-four.

The next weeks were full of much nausea and fatigue for me. My husband Doron was thrilled about the baby and I was prayerful that, when I felt better, I would not feel so overwhelmed.

I underwent an ultrasound at twelve weeks to rule out a prolapsed cervix. Seeing my baby's little arms and legs moving reminded me of the special life growing inside of me.

My attitude greatly improved and my nausea and fatigue decreased as I began my second trimester.

On November 24, I awoke to some blood clots. My doctor visit ruled it cervical bleeding and not a problem.

That night, I was cramping and passing more blood clots. I spent several hours in the E.R. and I was able to see my baby via ultrasound with a strong heartbeat and movement.

Doctors thought the small tear in my placenta would seal off and heal. I was told to see my regular doctor the next morning.

I went home and crawled in bed, exhausted from lack of sleep. But around 3:00 p.m. my cramps began again and by 11:00 p.m., I was in full labor.

Now we knew the miscarriage could not be stopped.

After a very hard contraction, we saw our fourteen week, five-inch-long baby boy. Doron carefully detached him from the threadlike umbilical cord, washed him, and prayed over him.

As we held his tiny body in our hands, we marvelled at how beautiful and perfect he was at only fourteen weeks! His little arms and hands lay folded on each side of his head. His fingers and toes were the size of pencil lead.

I understood in a new way the words of Psalm 139:14 that we are *"fearfully and wonderfully made."*

The doctor had been on the phone and heard all that went on as our baby was delivered. Doron requested a room for me at the hospital rather than E.R. again.

Doron also called a local funeral director who said he would meet us at the hospital to pick up our baby. We considered our little boy to be a precious life and we wanted to honor him as such.

Doron wept as he wrapped our baby in a washcloth, which he gently placed in the front pouch of his hoody.

The funeral director met us after midnight to pick up our precious jewel. He wrapped our little boy in a soft blue blanket and placed him in an urn within a small wooden box.

We buried him in a small grave beside my husband's granny. We named him Timothy David, which means "honored of God" and "beloved," but I shall always call him my "Tiny Tim."

My prayer is that God will receive glory for the wonder of an unborn baby and perhaps my testimony will save another baby's life.

Pencil sketch of
Timothy David Smith

Sheila (and Doron) Smith
Corbin, Kentucky

A Brief, Blessed Life

When my first daughter Karen was born, everything seemed normal. But, as Karen began to grow, I noticed she couldn't sit up without toppling over, and she wasn't learning to crawl like other babies.

At the University Hospital in Ann Arbor, Michigan, doctors discovered Karen had a muscular disorder. They said she would be in a wheelchair the rest of her life, and may not live to be more than seven years old.

Karen spent most of the day in a wheelchair when she wasn't laying down. She smiled a lot and was always very cheerful. She never felt sorry for herself or complained, even though she experienced a great deal of pain. Instead, she was always concerned for other people.

We moved to Flagstaff, Arizona, when Karen was sixteen. Now she was getting weaker all the time.

One day, a visiting nurse suggested I take her to a prayer meeting. There, we met many Spirit-filled believers from many denominations, and they willingly prayed for Karen and for me.

At this time, Karen became the first one in our family to give her heart to the Lord.

People from the prayer group would come to our house during the week to pray with Karen. She told everyone boldly, "The Lord is going to heal me and I'm going to spend the rest of my life serving Him and spreading the Gospel wherever He wants me to go."

Then a severe kidney infection put Karen in the hospital. While she was there, one of the prayer partners had a vision of her standing before the Lord with her arms uplifted (At this time, she couldn't raise her arms at all.) He thought the Lord must have taken her home, but when he phoned the hospital, they said Karen was fine.

He went to visit her the next day and asked, “Karen, did you feel anything different happen to you yesterday?”

With a smile, Karen closed her eyes. “Oh yes,” she said quietly. “I was lifted up to the Lord.”

She died a few days later at the age of seventeen. At her funeral, so many of her schoolmates and also other grownups came up and told me what a difference Karen had made in their lives. They said, if it hadn’t been for Karen’s kindness, love and giving of herself, their lives wouldn’t have been the same.

Karen truly did carry out the Lord’s work for as long as He gave her on this earth. And, in Heaven, I know she has experienced God’s healing touch on her body.

How I miss her, but I also rejoice in the knowledge that God blessed me with a special little girl for seventeen years.

Karen Hogan, born 2-19-56
Entered Heaven 12-13-1973

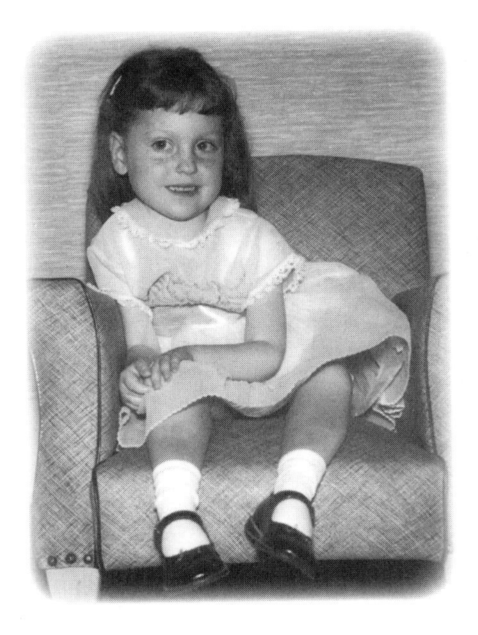

“Precious in the sight of the Lord is the death of His saints.”
Psalm 116:15

Margaret Rickard
Beaverton, Oregon

Beauty from Ashes

In an instant, my brother Bob Kirkland went from "riding high" as a respected and well-known horseman and civic leader at the peak of his productivity, to the devastation of being a quadriplegic, unable to even feed himself.

When a horse bucked Bob off during an afternoon trail ride, a portion of Bob's spine shattered. So did all his dreams.

Because he needed constant care for every detail of his life, Bob had to be placed in a foster care home.

Fighting discouragement and despair, he contacted my church for counseling. The pastors encouraged Bob to trust God in the midst of his anguish. One woman came to the foster care home each week to share God's Word with him.

A miracle unfolded as my active, self-sufficient brother slowed down and became a godly, praying person.

One day he told me, "Mabel, I'm glad God allowed this tragedy to happen because now I know the Lord. And the power of God has changed my life."

Bob took every opportunity to phone and befriend those in need. He especially uplifted people who suffered physical ailments. Often he would ride the Trimet disability bus to visit those in the hospital or confined at home.

A weekly expectation for literally scores of people was his encouraging phone call telling them, "I hope you have a wonderful weekend!"

I saw how God had used a crushing blow to remake my brother into a humble and loving servant of the Lord. Now, even though Bob was totally incapacitated, he used what he had—his voice—to bless others and glorify God.

During Bob's last hospitalization, after the doctors put him on a ventilator, our family gathered around his bedside to make the ultimate decision.

We asked Bob, "Do you want to have surgery that would leave you without a voice, but with a few more years to live?"

He shook his head, "No."

"Do you understand," I continued slowly, "that if they take you off the ventilator, you may not live very long. Are you ready to enter into the presence of the Lord?"

Bob nodded, "Yes."

So the doctors removed the ventilator. By evening, Bob's life had begun to ebb away.

As he neared the end of his life, I was privileged to hold his hands and pray with him: "Dear Lord, help Bob transition into Your Kingdom with joy and thanksgiving. Welcome him home. He has been such a faithful servant."

Shortly after that prayer, Bob's spirit left his crippled body. And I rejoiced in the miracle God had done to take my brother —reduced to nothingness—and rebuild the ashes of his life into a thing of great beauty.

As a mighty prayer warrior and personal encourager, he had touched the lives of a countless number of people.

"The Lord has sent Me to . . . comfort all who mourn . . . to give them beauty for ashes, the oil of joy for mourning."
Isaiah 61:1-3

Mabel Kirkland Ramsthel
Tigard, Oregon

In memory of
Robert "Bob" Kirkland
Entered Heaven 3-2-10

Appreciate Life

It's a shame that people, like me, sometimes have to go through a life–threatening experience before they develop a true appreciation for life and what it is all about.

In the late summer of 1991, I was slowed to a stop by severe pains in my lower abdomen for three days. A checkup at the hospital diagnosed "food poisoning," and they sent me home.

But, that afternoon, an aneurysm behind my heart caused me to pass out at home. My wife Georgia called 9-1-1.

When I regained consciousness a short time later, I saw a dozen paramedics and firefighters standing in my bedroom, and I realized they were all working on me!

Since they couldn't get an I.V. into my arteries, which had collapsed, I was rushed back to the hospital.

Soon I lay in intensive care with two pints of blood going into my arm.

That night, just five feet from the foot of my bed, I heard another family discuss with their doctor the possibilities of disconnecting life support tubes on their grandmother, who lay in the bed on the other side of the room.

Finally, doctors turned off the life support machines and the family members spent time saying good-bye to their precious mother and grandmother.

In my prayers, I asked the Lord to give all of them peace and comfort, and to receive this precious woman into His loving arms.

Then I asked, "Lord Jesus, why is all of this taking place right here in front of me?"

The Lord spoke clearly to me and said, "I want you, James, to enjoy life on earth while you have it. You will now know life more *abundantly.*"

Soon I fell asleep. When I woke up, two men arrived from the morgue to pick up the woman's body. They stopped near my bed for a few minutes to complete the paperwork for the hospital. The body was lying on the stretcher beside me.

"Why this, Lord? Why?" I asked.

"Today she is with Me in paradise," Jesus said. "Now you go forth to share My life with everyone you meet."

I lay there weeping after they had taken the dear lady's body away. As I quietly praised the Lord, my heart suddenly started racing on ahead of me so fast I couldn't keep up.

Then my heart stopped!

I was wired up to the monitors at the nurses' station, so the "code red" lit up their monitors. As beepers went off all around me, nurses and doctors came running.

While they were using the defibrillator paddles on me, a Voice spoke to me and said, "I am here, right here with you."

I responded, "Thank You, Lord. Praise Your name!"

The surgery on my heart was a success and I've had no problems with it since. Now, every day I live, I want to claim these words of Jesus and take Him up on His offer:

Jesus said, *"I have come that you might have life, and that you might have it more abundantly."* John 10:10

James "Jim" Allen, author
Send in the Clowns
Portland, Oregon

Journey of Faith

"Who among you fears the Lord?
Who obeys the voice of His Servant?
Who walks in darkness and has no light?
Let him trust in the name of the Lord
and rely upon his God.

Look, all you who kindle a fire,
who encircle yourselves with sparks;
Walk in the light of your fire
and in the sparks you have kindled
—This you shall have from My hand;
You shall lie down in torment."

Isaiah 50:10-11

The Lord promises:
"I will bring the blind by a way they did not know;
I will lead them in paths they have not known.
I will make darkness light before them,
and crooked places straight.
These things I will do for them,
and not forsake them."
Isaiah 42:16

We don't want to "light our own fires." But walking in the dark can be a challenging walk. Darkness demands that one must listen carefully and step forward boldly, yet with caution.

Trusting the Lord for the next step to take is never easy, but it will result in a far higher vision than we could ever have dreamed or imagined.

The following individuals who share their stories demonstrate the joy of walking by faith, not by sight.

In the Daily Miracle

It is so very assuring that I have traveled this road for over eighty years and still find God working tirelessly in my life, still bringing new revelations.

In these many years of raising a family, my wife and I have experienced repeated instances of God's grace, working to bring us all to maturity.

Many miracles involved new birth, near death, and insecurities where there seemed to be no good prospects. The solutions were all so profound that we could not count them as mere "accidents."

Over a period of time, I stuck these incidents in my pocket as living evidence of being loved and cared for by God, and I would pull them out periodically as dramatic reminders.

God could have left it at that, knowing that we "get it" without the daily, more subtle, incursions of the Holy Spirit.

God's real strength is always displayed in these daily blessings. I think that is so He would not be known as the great miracle-giver, but as the steadfast and ever-present Shepherd of our lives that He is.

It is in that daily anticipation of these mysteries that my faith has grown, and not just in the profoundly dramatic ones that blow me away.

At one time, I would have smiled (like sometimes we smile away things we don't understand) at the thought of actually *hearing* God's voice.

I had never experienced it and I did not believe it. At the same time, I believed God could and would communicate to me somehow.

My conception back then was that God's voice would always

be audible. But now I know it is His Spirit in me who uses daily circumstances to direct, reward, challenge and make my life a joy to live.

There is not a day now that I don't hear His voice in my soul, especially in the many things *We* write and the art *We* create together.

In the escape from my own folly and selfishness as I grow older, each move on His part is an endorsement that I sorely need.

And, at a time when my purpose might falter or disappear, I look at those vested gifts in terms of the responsibility connected with them, as was His intent. I know that my life's purpose is secure forever.

"For God's gifts and His call are irrevocable.
He never withdraws them once they are given,
and He does not change His mind about those to whom
He gives grace; or to whom He sends His call."

Romans 11:29

Milt Wear
Artist, author & poet
www.christianblog.com
Beaverton, Oregon

God's Royal Priest

I love the picture of Aaron, the High Priest, standing before the Lord, as he entered the Holy of Holies in the Temple once a year on the Day of Atonement.

Aaron stood in God's presence, bearing the names of the twelve tribes of Israel on his heart. Aaron wore a breastplate woven with gold, blue, purple and scarlet thread on fine linen cloth.

Twelve precious stones were set in gold settings on the priest's breastplate: a ruby, a topaz, an emerald, a turquoise, a sapphire, a diamond, an amber, an agate, an amethyst, a beryl, an onyx, and a jasper.

Each stone was engraved with the name of one of Jacob's twelve children: Reuben, Simeon, Levi, Judah, Issachar, Zebulun, Dan, Gad, Asher, Naphtali, Joseph, and Benjamin.

We read God's instructions in Exodus 28:29:

"So Aaron shall bear the names of the sons of Israel (the new name God gave to Jacob) on the breastplate of judgment over his heart, when he goes into the holy place, as a memorial before the Lord continally."

I picture myself, as a member of God's royal priesthood, standing in front of the Lord in prayer.

On my heart, I carry the precious jewels which the Lord has entrusted to me.

These "jewels" are my children, my grandchildren, my great-grandchildren, and my whole extended family.

I present my family to the Lord daily, not just once a year. Unlike Aaron, who had to make a sacrifice for his own sin before he entered into God's presence, I can enter into God's presence at anytime because of the "once for all" sacrifice Jesus made on the cross for me.

As I bring before the Lord my loved ones inscribed on my heart and my lips, *"[The Lord] will be reminded of His people continually"* (Exodus 28:29 NLT).

What a great privilege to stand in God's presence on behalf of my loved ones, my precious jewels!

Maybe that's the work God has for me to do now, and the reason why He has not taken me to my home in heaven yet. You think so?

"But you are a chosen generation,
a royal priesthood . . .
that you may proclaim the praises of Him
who called you out of darkness
into His marvelous light."
1 Peter 2:9

Margie Vannoy
King City, Oregon

Past, Present, Future

My wife and I experienced firsthand in Holland what it was like to live under the occupation of a foreign nation who robbed us of our freedom.

With our three-month-old twin boys, we came to America in 1961 with two suitcases and $90.00.

We learned to love this country and the great people who live here. We appreciated the opportunities we were given to be successful in family and business.

Many stories could be written about our family and about our business ventures through fifty years of ups and downs, of successes and failures. We started our own business, knocking on doors to sell plants and landscape work.

Up to a few years ago, we grew and raised a family, and, together with the Lord, built a most successful business. We employed many people, and our jobs took us from Alaska to Southern Oregon. We shipped nursery stock to the East Coast and Canada. Most of our clients were local landscape architects and designers, developers and contractors.

Today, we see many changes in our country, and in people.

Where is my focus today in these most difficult days? When sitting behind my desk early mornings with bills to be paid and a desk full of papers, they draw me away from reading and praying. And God seems far away.

Our children, with the exception of one, have little interest in the Lord or church. Our grandchildren have no interest or time to respond to God's calling. It hurts, but I must be honest. Did I read the Word in my early days?

In the past few years, unpurchased trees in our nursery have grown so big that nobody can afford to buy them. The labor and equipment needed to transport them cost too much. As they have become too large to transplant, we've had to burn an untold number of trees and also numerous overgrown plants.

Now there is no construction, no landscaping, sales are down. We laid off many of our workers. Wages are reduced.

The most difficult part of all is that we do not have any answers! And it is not only the economy; it touches all areas. The life-sustaining building blocks are cracking.

Am I too cynical? I don't think so.

What is our future? That depends.

When I reach the end and I don't have an answer, and I feel the heat of the fires burning in the nursery, I must find the answers in God's Word—that is my Source.

Then I find strength and comfort because the prophet Micah recorded these words 2,710 years ago, for me and for all of us:

"And He, Jesus, shall stand and feed his flock in the strength of the Lord, in majesty of the name of the Lord,
His God, and His people shall remain there undisturbed,
for He will be greatly honored all around the world.
HE will be our PEACE!"

Micah 5:4-5 *(paraphrase)*

Fred (and Carla) Meisner
Cascadian Nurseries, Hillsboro, Oregon

Power in a Few Words

I stayed overnight in a motel south of Indianapolis, Indiana, on a trip to Detroit, Michigan, to visit family. In the morning, I ate breakfast at the motel restaurant.

Afterwards, I talked with the waitress who gave me back my credit card. After I signed the receipt and handed it over to her, I asked, "Do you need prayer for anything?"

She sadly brushed aside a tear as she answered, "Oh, yes! My twenty-three-year-old daughter has moved back in with me. She doesn't have a job and she hangs around drug users. I don't know what I'm going to do with her."

Tears welled up in her eyes as she added, "And I have an uncle who is dying of cancer. He's terminal," she told me in a depressed tone of voice.

"I feel overwhelmed," she added, "and I don't have a church home."

I heard myself say, "I'll put you on my prayer list and I'll pray for you."

Six months later, I purposely chose that same route to drive to Michigan, stayed in the same motel, and ate breakfast at the same restaurant.

When I came to pay my bill, I asked the waitress, "How's your life been going lately?"

With a smile on her face, she told me excitedly, "I have other customers also praying for me now, and things are much better, thank you!"

After a short conversation, I left the restaurant feeling like the question, "Do you need prayer for anything?" definitely made a difference in one person's life.

On a later trip to Michigan, I came back to the same restaurant and checked with the waitress once again.

"How's your life been going lately?" I asked.

She cheerfully reported, "Everything is going much better! I've found a friendly church where I have so much support. Thank you again for taking time to support me in your prayers."

Her face it up as she told me, "By the way, my daughter now has a job and she no longer hangs out with the drug crowd. She has even moved into her own apartment."

As I left the restaurant and walked to my car, I couldn't help but reflect:

What power there is in a few simple words spoken in deep concern, like the words:

"Do you need prayer for anything?"

"We, being many, are one body in Christ . . .
[continue] steadfastly in prayer . . .
Rejoice with those who rejoice,
and weep with those who weep."
Romans 12: 5, 12, 15

Norman Borsvold
Beaverton, Oregon

One Plants, One Waters

As I was strolling in the park one day, I noticed an older lady standing on a platform at the edge of the lake.

I asked the Lord: "Do you want me to speak to her?"

The reply was: *"Go ye into all the world, and preach the Gospel to every creature"* Mark 16:15 (KJV).

I soon discovered that she had been a child during the time of Hitler's Germany—a time when thousands of Bibles were burned, including her family Bible, and when many preachers preached only the 'party' line.

Although she was a church goer, she said she had never received the Lord as her personal Savior. She still was not open to this, even after I talked with her for an hour.

As I recall, I gave her a Bible and encouraged her to check out a particular church.

A few years later I met her again and she was still "floating."

St. Paul wrote, *"I have planted, Apollos watered; but God gave the increase"* (1 Corinthians 3:6 KJV).

God is in charge. I entrust her to His care. I have prayed for her salvation and for Christians to come along side her. I have no reservations about speaking to people. His command and His desire say it all.

"This is good, and pleases God our Savior, who wants all men to be saved and to come to a knowledge of the truth."
1 Timothy 2:3-4 (NIV)

Len Hutchinson
Beaverton, Oregon

Walk in the "Dark"

In 1969 when we spent three weeks in Switzerland at L'Abri, Dr. Francis Schaeffer encouraged David and me to walk in faith *"in the dark,"* holding God's hand (Isaiah 50:10-11).

Returning to the USA, we began—in faith—to step forward into unknown paths as we felt God call David to work as an artist. But we didn't know if he could make a living as a painter.

David's father reacted negatively. "Go get a ***real*** job!" he said.

But we decided to move ahead as the Lord showed us. We knew that, if we were faithful to do God's will, then everything would work out for His glory and for our good.

As we prayed, God helped us hear His voice, catch His vision and trust Him to lead and provide. Our lives became an "object lesson" of God's faithful care for all our "needs."

For years, I mailed monthly mortgage checks and payments on utility bills, even though there weren't enough funds in our bank account. Then a painting would sell at exactly the right time to cover those checks when they arrived at our bank.

The checks never bounced . . . except once. The day we received the bank's pink slip, I wondered: *Why has God failed to meet our needs?* Then, I discovered it was MY fault. A check for the sale of one of David's paintings ***had*** arrived on time in the mail, but I had waited 'til the next day to deposit it!

In forty-three years of marriage, we've had only four years of employment income. God has proved Himself faithful and helped us write and illustrate fifty-five books. Even today, God still helps us overcome fear by keeping our eyes focused on *Him.*

"Lord, we don't know what to do, but our eyes are on You."
2 Chronicles 20:12

Helen & David Haidle
Tigard, Oregon

Write Your Memorials

"Then those who feared the LORD
spoke to one another,
and the LORD listened and heard them;
So a bookof remembrance was written [in his presence]
for those who fear the LORD
and who meditate on His name.

"They shall be Mine," says the LORD of hosts,
"On the day when I make up them My jewels.
And I will spare them, as a man spares
his own son who serves him."

Malachi 3:16-17

Hopefully your own awareness of God's work in your life has been heightened as you have read through these stories.

Perhaps some almost-forgotten incidents have resurfaced and returned to your memory.

Take time to make notes on your memories. You can always finish writing your stories at a later time.

Just don't do what many people have done:

Don't take "your book" to heaven with you!

Don't leave this earth without letting others know the times and events where God was at work in your life.